The Careless
Embrace
of the
Boneshaker

great
weather
for

Printed in the United States of America

First Edition
ISBN: 978-0-9857317-9-3
Library of Congress Control Number: 2016908969

Editors: Jane Ormerod, Thomas Fucaloro, David Lawton, George Wallace, Russ Green
Guest Prose Editor: Thaddeus Rutkowski

Book design: Jane Ormerod
Cover photograph: Amy Bassin
Photograph of Thurston Moore: Phil Sharp

great weather for MEDIA, LLC
New York, NY

www.greatweatherformedia.com

The Careless
Embrace
of the
Boneshaker

great weather for MEDIA

New York City

CONTENTS

176 Contributors

INTRODUCTION

Welcome to great weather for MEDIA's fifth anthology of poetry and short prose. If last year's *Before Passing* mixed memory and anticipation, *The Careless Embrace of the Boneshaker* rattles and rises. Here are writers claiming who they are and screaming it from the top of their lungs. They are the boneshakers. Each one of them. Like the 19th century bicycle prototype from which they get their name, they have no means of shock absorption. They accept the random and unanticipated jolts they meet on the road of life. That might leave them lifelessly laid out on top of a mound of garbage, or up all night enumerating the minutes since they have fallen hopelessly in love. That drains the identity away through the lines in a grandmother's hands, and inspires catlike reflexes on the hardtop streets of Brooklyn. Even the jarring impact of reliving someone else's trauma, and feeling it is also your own. This is how they help us understand who we are by letting us understand who they are. From Taylor Steele to John W. Snyder to Janet Hamill, these poems erupt with a sense of empowerment.

And, as our journey has continued, we gather new friends along the way. From England to Philadelphia, Los Angeles to Seattle, the Rainbow Book Fair to the New York City Poetry Festival, our community grows. In January we hosted a very special spoken word event with Thurston Moore and we are thrilled to include an interview with Thurston in this book.

In addition, we published two more single poet collections: *Harvest the Dirt* by Wil Gibson and *Exercises in High Treason* by John J. Trause. Upcoming books include *Crown Prince of Rabbits* by John Paul Davis, due this fall. We are proud too of recent successes enjoyed by our authors. Corrina Bain's collection *Debridement* was a finalist for The Publishing Triangle Award for Trans and Gender-Variant Literature, and Puma Perl was a recipient of a 2016 Acker Award for achievement in the avant garde. From *Before Passing*, Britt Haraway and Eliel Lucero's works were selected for inclusion in *The Best Small Fictions 2016* anthology published by Queen's Ferry Press. Congratulations to all!

It is also a time of editorial change. Russ Green is moving to new challenges and study. We are hugely appreciative of his work here. Russ is passionate for poetry and we wish him well. Moving forward, we will be graced by two new editors: Aimee Herman and Mary McLaughlin Slechta.

We wish to express our deepest gratitude to our guest prose editor Thaddeus Rutkowski for his enthusiasm and skilled selection. Like our previous anthologies, we do not look for a theme and our writers come from numerous backgrounds and experiences. From widely published to first time in print, we love the way these writers surprise us. Special thanks also to our cover artist Amy Bassin. These writers reveal, disguise, play, and tear away. Words on paper, paper on face. What do you wish to see? How much can you take?

So, take heed and follow the embrace of the boneshaker. Let the impact wrap itself around you.

Birth Certificate

JANET HAMILL

My birth certificate reads   substitution bird destined to walk upright

against her will   against prohibitive tickets to flying feats   of black doves

similarly immobilized   with six-foot wing spans   spanning continents

a-go-go   a bowling green   & shadows cast in mercury   glass her eye

balls   holding secrets of the intricate bone structure   of spirit mazes

The Linen Spells

SARA FETHEROLF

There is a spell to find the right road, to see
in the dark and to pass by day without being seen.
There are spells for not letting a man's head be
cut off, spells for bringing stone animals to life
and for making them plow. For cultivating
and for murder, for seeing far, for traveling by flight.

Oh so-and-so, the spells go.

Oh so-and-so, oh sod god,
oh villain, oh charmer, oh card cheat.
Oh weigher of hearts and changer
of sheets. Oh good host,
oh blood-on-the-teeth, oh endless &c.

She who breaks the necks of kittens. He who overwaters the roses.
Oh stranger. Oh thief.

There's a spell to trick the judges, a spell to pass safely over water, and, failing
all else, the spell of transformation, which can change the beloved dead
to a creature that enters
the underworld unnoticed.

Oh snake, oh feline. Oh long spine, oh thing that senses the future through its nose-tip.
Let me not lose a word of it. Let me slither on through.

All These Bodies

TAYLOR STEELE

Another black boy got killed today
And he was my brother   but not
And he was my son   if
there is a word for being rebirthed unborn
If   he can have not been yet   and just have been   at the same

Another black girl got killed today
And she was sick   like me
                              I
got killed today if there is a word for being in this body alive but also in another body
to feel another body lose its body and to return to one's own alive but knowing death
now like a thing it lived through because it did

Another black <u>fill in the blank</u> got killed today
Is there a word for reliving someone else's trauma but also it is your trauma because
your body is still everyone else's body even when you are alone even when your mother
tells you you came out of her you know you also came out of so many other dark
holes and you remember the casket as a door to a room you were told never to go in
even though your name is etched into its wood like an incantation is there a word
for that   for

                              I cried for an hour yesterday because America is the
                              loneliest angry song I've ever heard and once knew all
                              the words to

Is there a word for that
For forgetting a song

Is there a word for forgetting when you've forgotten the word itself just remember
mourning this thing you knew once the way you know how to hold your breath and
you hold your breath in your body and inhale in another and suddenly a dead black <u>fill</u>
<u>in the blank</u> is alive again but really it is just you not having died yet and the world sighs
relieved because it knows you will die soon anyway because what is a black body but
not a body at all just maybe air just maybe a pinky promise white supremacy outgrew
just maybe the seeing of a hunter his rifle the forest the deer the sign that says it is not
hunting season seeing the hunter his rifle the forest the dead deer   maybe that is it
but that's not a word
Is there a word for that for being the thing that sees without a body to see through for
being a thing for being black is there a word in American for   that

Tripping

ED TONEY

I run fast, a jaguar, trip over an 8½ by 11 piece
of beige cheap bond paper and as always, skin my tongue

Blood over Sudan, Congo wars, no mercy
my jugular rips, my bleeding words spill, a blood imagery

my eyes are blind, but talkative
tell me, does this reason the rhyme or scorch the pot

did that child with a student visa
just aim a crockpot at me. Is this Boston or Istanbul

A B C, he learns but to pray is what he means
I run again, trip, just fell in a pile of burning poems

I am a burning volcano
my gut stinks, my esophagus tall and onyx like the Sphinx

Is there a White Castle, I mean a white house on this street
I got the crave, a craving for the truth, but this grease is a lie

Is there a mathematician, a time traveler "of color" I can talk to
Ask her or him to calculate the distance traveled B.efore C.hrist

Aliens, please! Fuck that shit, there is no such thing. that's me! that's us! why won't all of "them" just accept the fact we have always been here

for a very long time, since the very beginning!

I of the Beholder

DAVID ROY LINCOLN

The first corpse appeared one day outside Ratna Park. It was nudged up on a mound of rotting vegetable matter, no sign of a struggle, only that peaceful stiffness in the arms and legs. The clothes were hardly wrinkled, the man might have reclined to take a nap and drifted off, with a little smile on his face. Every so often pedestrians tossed a coin over the remains. One and two rupee donations were piling up nearby like he might have hoped for when he was alive and—too late—the windfall was building up with a kind of dead man scatter, like a drawing I once made with a stencil.

I was speeding through at a decent clip on my green Chinese bicycle, and the glimpse of (unmistakably) an empty body blurring by at the corner of my eye, prompted me to hop off. This was exciting. I had never seen an empty body in the flesh. It was just unmoving and rested on top of its own little mountain of coconut hulls, smeary plastic bags, rice-mucked banana leaves, yesterday's salad fare, a cosmic laughter captured in the face somewhere. I wasn't comfortable looking at it directly but, despite a certain hardening of appearance, I noticed a turning up of the lips.

A random stray goat was nibbling at the edge of the vegetables right now. Suddenly I thought I could make out the last thought, clinging on in the corner of his eye like a wet spot, at the deepest level in his gaze, which was still directed out at the street. I tilted my head to line up with his head and gazed into the back of his right eye, which was still lucid, to see if there was anything like a final comment that may have lingered there. With a shock I noticed, inside a soft yellow glimmer, the face of a man peering back at me, as through a cracked-open door in that retina. In fact, a tiny diorama at the back of his brain dramatically rendered the smog-smuggered capitol, the mass of traffic sliding against itself, hordes of black smoke-belching buses and Tata trucks, and streams of brightly dressed young people parading around in their finest city impressions. The man just remained like he was not giving in to the temptation to itch his leg or something. He might have been staring off like that for a while, the whole world just turning around at the edge of his vegetable plot.

Maybe he had watched me biking past the Bhimsen Tower every day for the last three weeks around noon, I realized. I always came through cranking madly, my dark hair flying, my shoulders and face exerting themselves with a radiance and the sweat staining down the back of my thin cotton kurta as I leaned into the lugubrious one-speed. I would have presented the pale vision of someone from another culture, working, like . . . like an engine, I thought. I would have been embarrassed to always be the one blurring by in the background on my way to some important shift, always in a panic. This one had nothing but time on his hands, his body did not shift noticeably, probably ever. He might have even asked himself who was that with the ponytail flashing by in a terrible blur all the time? Maybe I thought tomorrow might never come? Maybe I had to get to my office and there was this thing we believed in in my country, an abstraction called time, as if somehow reality was not the same later in the day? Maybe this man intuited something about me, say he had escaped from a remote village in the mountains, and he came to the big city to find his goals, and there I was, and he felt better about himself. Not what he had expected, I would expect. Was I a stranger? Was he under a false impression?

I had left my suburb too, and until recently I was poor, the differences between us were not so much. I would have agreed, at least, what an odd sight I had become. If our roles were reversed, we could have compared notes and talked late into the night, and supported each other, and dug up what I would never get around to doing, or what he had done that I admired. After that, neither of us would have expected to feel alone ever again. I did not know Indo-Tibetan or Gurung-ese, or whatnot ethnic language he spoke, but this man could have sympathized with me, I felt, this wild one with the ranging black hair and simple wool red robe and plastic black sandals that had slipped off one foot, most likely when he gave up the ghost. At least our conversation would have been carried out in mutual respect, and maybe illuminated the twists and turns that brought us both to Kathmandu. Our conversation might have incited me to get out of bed in the morning. Was that an all-day smile? This went beyond place, I might add, our friendship would have located something, say it created solace in a world of personal detachment, and he had nothing left to do. Leave the amazement to all the others rushing around with their incredible burdens and inexhaustible stress and time management problems.

I only wished that he had not seen me first.

To signal my respect, I wanted to do something. There were no emergency lights or response teams wailing around the corner, like at home, no sirens or theater of lights slipping up the sides of the buildings. There wasn't even a smell. Hindus are a superlatively practical people and understand exactly how far apart to place their temples so the mind stays perfumed with kind thoughts all day, from the incense; smoke was curling in from the baths at Sundara, not far away. Had someone pushed him up the mound later, or had he himself climbed up, put his hands under his head, like it was a pillow, and slipped away into the dream?

Whatever the case, he was not bad looking, for a corpse.

I thrust my hand into a pocket, I pulled out whatever coins were available, and threw them from my fist without looking first, like they were flower petals sprinkled over the flat of his chest. Sooner or later, with the help of others, a rickshaw driver would appear and accept the humble commission and haul him away to the river. Whoever set the fire under him ought to maintain a little distance, I wanted to say, to protect his dignity. Which you could still make out plastered on his face, a leftover grin like a parting shot with the message still contained there, what he really thought about this all.

A Brief History of Every Internet Argument Ever

BRENDAN GILLETT

The sound of special
two-cent pennies in
a shiny blender
rattling so loud
that the glowing decals
threaten to fall off
and reveal the old
mechanics
gears made of stone
and fossilized intentions.

As the pennies tornado,
the questions:
will it blend
or
will they carry
or
will everyone remember
which penny they threw
in the first place?

The motor stops
from neglect.
The blender opens with
a whiff of raw copper.
The pennies
are scratched but
mostly from the blending.
Occasionally,
a little piece of one
will embed itself in
another

sometimes a rejected sliver
sometimes smelted
into the original
as the face is reshaped.

And it's funny;
the newest pennies
shine the brightest
but scratch the best.
The middlest pennies
have been calcified
by battle.
And the oldest pennies
become worn and green
until they are
almost unrecognizable
until they are
kind of like
the pennies
they used to argue with.

Another Those Mornings

DAN RAPHAEL

something the stomach wants and has no word for
waking beneath a sky its never seen, a sleeping bag of questionable origin:
could be a field with no visible buildings, could be a park next to morning traffic

haven't learned how they say hungry here, where do i recycle
whatever i drank to have this brilliant a headache
as various parts of my brain blame each other for this situation

a faucet without handles, a sink i cant reach the bottom of
the whistling of steam that's a parrot changing channels
to become a forecast of pale green sky and clouds as layered as shale

the weather woman comes in the back door with a basket of purple tomatoes
and 3 cucumbers that havent stopped dancing—i feel the bass in the floor
through my suddenly handsome feet as if a roller belt of sand rippling regular
to strengthen my legs and spine, bring my head closer to the ceiling fan
of muscular arms & flamingo necks—

                              the only way to stop spinning
is sit on a bar stool salvaged from this towns oldest tavern
before the meteor struck it but i cant pay the cover charge as my wallets
in that sleeping bag unzipping to its next assignment

First Fight

CECILY SCHULER

You ever just // sat // and watched // an alligator // steal her happy // ass // some sun //
for hours // on a bed // of flattened sawtooth // did you know // the spines on her back
// evolutionary // heat sinks // they come born // drinking radiation // did you know //
they come born // this or that gender // depending on the year // ('s) // season // (al) //
temperature // and their fate // (d) // placement within the nest // did you know // they
come born // with a tiny tooth // dorsal on the snout tip // that they must drag // across
the inside // of their leather casing // over and over // they must get strong // enough //
to rip // leather // to claw // thrash through their squirm // of siblings // route // through
detritus // their mama stamped down solid // around their shells // to protect them // but
also // to make them // fight for it // that their first fight is being // born // did you know //
they come born // grinning

Maybe When Your Daddy Strikes It Rich

ERIK IPSEN

Where I grew up in Alaska in the winter, even in the middle of the day we had to use a flashlight to read the thermometer hanging out on the side of the garage. Many days though, there was no point. The device was a fancy brass thing with a shiny blue-black arrow that swung in an arc from -20 to 110 degrees. My Aunt Helga, a sixth-grade teacher down in Sacramento, sent it to my dad as a late Christmas present our first year in that house.

The problem was that the dial started way too late since some days it could get down to 60 below out by us, and that's without the wind chill. What I'm trying to tell you is that Larry—that's my dad—was crazy. Crazy with greed would be more like it. That's what many people came to say in the years afterwards anyway. How else could anybody explain why he'd plucked his young family out of a nice warm place like Sacramento and dragged them all the way to Fairbanks like he did. At the time, I had just turned eleven, my five brothers and sisters ranged from six months to eight years, and our mom Lynn was already coughing up blood at night. Actually, we didn't even live in the city, we lived thirty-five miles north by the side of the State Highway 2, which in another few miles crosses the Yukon River on its way on to Dead Horse up on Prudhoe Bay. We lived way out there because nobody in their right mind wanted to live that far outa town, so the place was dirt cheap, and because it was close to the claim my dad bought from his cousin Jimmy.

He actually had two claims of forty acres each for which Jimmy told my dad he'd paid the government a grand total of $200. What got my dad's attention was the fire-engine-red Pontiac GTO that Jimmy showed up driving in Sacramento early one autumn and his story about how he'd struck it rich up in Alaska. Turns out that after digging and blasting for six years and getting nowhere, Jimmy turned to panning and—whaddyaknow—

he'd ended up finding nearly twenty ounces of gold in two blessed months before the snow returned. Jimmy, though, said he was tired of Alaska, of the bugs and bears in the summers, the cold in the winter, and the loneliness all the time.

And that's how it was that Dad agreed to pay Jimmy $10,000 for a half share of his claims and to split all future profits sixty for Jimmy and forty for Dad, who was going to be doing all the work while Jimmy looked to start a family down in sunny California.

And that's how we came by our little house along the highway on a ten acre parcel of what my mom called "nothing." The lot sloped gently upwards towards the ridge line to the west where my dad had what he called his "gold mine," and what Mom called "the pit." And that's about it. As for our land, I have to say Mom was kinda right. There were no trees, no trails, no ponds, no nothing, just a lifetime supply of moss, lichen. Even the moose and the caribou knew better than to come scrounging around our place for anything more than a light snack. Oddly enough, my mom wrote to her best friend Peggy Epstein after the first snowfall in September of our second year and confessed that she was looking forward to winter. In the letter Mom explained that no light for weeks on end allowed her to return to what she called a "visual void." It was a time when her imagination was freed to run completely wild over that barren landscape and with the help of the aurora borealis to make of it in her mind's eye something truly awesome—a phantasmagorical world that constantly took on wild hues and shapes. That second winter though is when her cough began to get worse, and the pile of bloody paper towels in the bin grew much higher. More than once I told Mom she oughta go to the doctor, but each time she just patted me on the head and said the exact same thing: "Maybe when your daddy strikes it rich, honey, we'll have money for such things."

That's also when she started to get a kind of faraway look in her pale blue eyes, so striking even the little kids used to whisper: "Mommy's gone off to Mars." She also started humming to herself a lot, always the same three mid-range notes that she finished off with a long low one that hinted at the end of hope.

We'd moved up there, of course, in the summer. Even my dad had enough sense not to try it in the winter, which began to tiptoe in just after Labor Day.

At first all us kids thought Alaska might be kinda fun. With sun all day long and temperatures that could stretch to a hundred, the place was a dream, especially since

Fairbanks had a great pool in the park down by the Chena River. Each of those light-choked days went on so long that even the plants kinda flipped out. They got so ginormous, you'd have thought there was some sort of nuke plant nearby or something. Little marigold plants like I'd grown up with in Sacramento, in Fairbanks became massive mounds of orange and yellow with more blossoms than we had on all the marigolds in our whole neighborhood back at home, which was a lot. And the cabbage that many folks grew to get themselves through the winter with vegetables? Those things got to be two feet tall and nearly five feet wide, so big people had to cut them up into pieces with saws just to get 'em into the house.

Anyway when fall came, my dad went back to being a plumber. Back to actually making some money, as Mom put it. He worked for a friend of his cousin Jimmy. His name was Pete, and his trucks all had a big gold crown painted on the side—which was about the only gold my dad ever saw. Underneath that crown it said, *Pete Reimschneider, Fairbanks' Prince of Pipes & Plumbing.* Each morning Dad would load me and my three oldest brothers and sisters into his old dark-green Ford Bronco and drop us at school on his way into work, leaving my mom and the two little ones at home in our three-room log cabin which—did I mention—didn't have electricity? Anyway, it didn't. It was supposed to. Even my dad wasn't dumb enough to buy a house that didn't have power in the middle of someplace where nights drag on for weeks and where people can get snowed in for days. The realtor who sold us the house mentioned five times that Alaska Power & Light was rolling a line out in our direction and promised it'd only be "a matter of weeks" before we got hooked up and "the juice" would flow through all the wires we had ready and waiting in our walls and ceilings. But it never did, not in the two and a half years that my mom lived there, at least.

Funny thing was that everything all kind of collapsed in on itself in early April of what would have been our third year, just when the sun was actually beginning to warm things up. It happened just a couple of days after little Roy's third birthday. We got home from town, where Dad had taken me and the three older kids to see "Ben Hur," and discovered that they were gone. Chrissy, age five, was all tucked into her bed, sound asleep with a bad cold. But Mom and Roy weren't anywhere. By then it was pitch dark. Dad went out and called and called. "Lih-inn, Row-oyy; Lih-inn, Row-oyy." Then he came back in, and without saying anything strapped on his snow shoes, grabbed his big flashlight, and ran out the door. Later, he told the police that he'd seen a single set of tracks leading away from the back of the house heading towards the ridge.

As it turned out they hadn't gotten very far. It'd been just a few degrees below zero that afternoon, but although Mom had bundled Roy up tight, she hadn't even bothered to change her slippers for boots much less put a coat on. She was ice cold by the time dad found her in the snow with her arms wrapped tightly around little Roy, still alive. Dad told the police he'd had to break one of mom's arms to free him. Clutching Roy close to his chest inside his coat, Dad ran back into the house, shouted to me to watch the others, jumped into the Bronco, and barreled off.

It wasn't until I'd put the kids to bed that I heard a knock on the door. It was Officer Knudson, whose son Glenn was in my class at school. He had me wake up the kids, even Chrissy, who remember was sick, and then told us all that our mom was "gone" as he put it. But he told us Roy would be fine after awhile. That's when Chrissie finally broke down and started crying, and we all joined in, even Officer Knudson who had a reputation as kind of a tough guy.

Late the next morning, Dad came home with a far-away look in his eyes kind of like Mom's Martian one. Without taking off his coat, he stood in the center of the room and told us "your beautiful mother has gone away forever." As for little Roy, it turned out Officer Knudson was not totally right. Dad said Roy's feet and legs were badly frostbitten.

A couple of days later we visited him in the hospital. He was asleep and had a little tent rigged up over his legs. In the end his doctors had to amputate his left leg at the knee and his right just above the ankle. In all, Roy spent nearly three weeks in that place. After that, we all stayed in the house for ten more days until our Aunt Helga came to take us back to Sacramento. That day in mid June was the last time any of us ever laid eyes on our dad or even heard from him. Nearly twenty-five years went by before I got a call from Glenn Knudson, my old Fairbanks classmate. Turns out he'd done what I'd done and followed in his dad's footprints by becoming a police officer, just like I'd done by going into the plumbing field. It was Sunday, June 2nd, and Sergeant Knudson was on the line with a bit of bad news. A hunter had found human remains face up in the snow a few hundred yards out back of our old house on Highway 2. Weirdly, the corpse had no clothes on much less ID. But it was still recognizable. It was Lawrence Albert Sweet. But just to make sure the authorities asked me to supply a sample of my "genetic material" so they could do a test. Before Glenn hung up, he paused for a long moment and then in a lowered voice filled in some of the blanks I hadn't had the courage to ask about.

"I'm not sure you want to know this Norm, but for the record our coroner concluded that your dad left the house naked, probably some time back in early spring, and died of hypothermia very shortly thereafter. That timing would fit with the last reported sighting anyone had of him. It came just after 1:00 p.m. on April 3, when he let a crew from APL into the house so they could bring power in from the road. Can you believe it took them all that damn time to hook you up? Anyway, Norm, I'm real sorry."

Of course, I told my brothers and sisters everything, except about Dad having been found naked. I speculated that he must have had a heart attack or something. Anyway, in the end the only one of us who wanted to fly up and collect the body was Roy, who works for Amazon up in Seattle handling customer complaints. He and our Aunt Helga went up together. They rented a helicopter and scattered Dad's ashes over where they figured his mine had been, but having never laid eyes on it themselves that was impossible to say. Frankly, I wonder if anybody could have done any better. I think the mine was always more of a dream than a real thing, at least the sort that would impress anybody.

Sublunary

CHRIS STEWART

Sublunary position,
A field of dead animals.
Half-Earth along the western quarterly,
In London it is 6 a.m.

_____*radio static*_____

He has lived his life like radio static,
As if his thoughts ought to come from elsewhere.
He talked out of step,
Like a scrambled radio transmission

ro_ fo___ _ea crea____rain___.
lu___sha___ in __rk___, o____ious ___ Plu __.
the ___rth ___ fou__ to __ the ___me __n _ime _ll _round.
___ sun ___ se _1_2 _rs ___rador
__the ___stern ___st __p,
____all ___clo___ say _____,
Lai___'s ___fin ___fts.

He is a jamming signal.
A silent moon in the penumbra.

                                    __ck __rm s__ ____tures ____bow.
                       __nar ____dow __ da__ness, _bliv____ 0f ___to.
                       __ea__ is ___nd __ be ___ sa__ su_ t___ a__ a
                                          The ___ ro__ 1_/_b__ Lab
                                     At ____ ea_____ mo___ ti_,
                               Where ____ the ___cks ____ night,
                                       __ka__ cof___ dri___.

UFO off port bow,
Alien capsule.
Transmission intercepted.

ro___ fo__ _ea crea____ rain___.
lu___sha____ in __rk____, o_____ious ___ Plu___. __ck __rm s__ ____tures ____bow.
    the__rth _ fou__ to __ the _me __n _ime _ll _round. _nar __dow __da__ness,
_bliv____ 0f ___to.

___ sun ___se _1_2 _rs ___rador___ ea__ is ___nd _ be ___ sa__su_ t___ a__ a_____
__the ___stern __st ___p, The__ ro__ 1_/_b__ Lab_____
____all ___ clo___ say _____, At ___ ea_____ mo___ ti_,
Lai___'s ___fin ____fts. Where ___ the ____cks ___night,
                                        ___ka__ cof__ dri___.

We hear a song,
A duet in the penumbra.

rock form sea creatures rainbow.
lunar shadow in darkness, oblivious of Pluto.
the earth is found to be the same sun time all around.

The sun rose 1 1/2 hrs Labrador
at the eastern most tip,
where all the clocks say night,
Laika's coffin drifts.

Then it came,
His first and last clear transmission.

Beneath the work of an earthquake,
The Pacific sweeps igneous tremors under the sea.
It is 7 AM BST in London,
And dawn will reach Brazil within the hour.

Collision imminent.

Roger. We await your oscillatory orbits.

In a sublunary position
Their castles kiss.

_____
_____
_____
_____
_____
_____
_____
_____
__

Radio silence.

INTERVIEW

I Look for Where the Poetry Is

THURSTON MOORE IN CONVERSATION WITH GEORGE WALLACE

A MUSICIAN WHO WRITES POETRY?

George Wallace: Let's get something out of the way right off the bat. Some people will identify you as a punk rocker first, and only secondarily as a poet. Is that fair? Is it accurate?

Thurston Moore: I guess I'm perennially cast as the musician playing while a poet reads. That's a certain factor I find difficult to deal with because it's a bit of a devaluation of the intention I have of being a poet. When you're preoccupied with music, especially, people tend to think "well maybe what you have is simply a dalliance with poetry." In fact, at an early age I wanted to move to New York and be a poet. But I was in love with rock and roll too, so I thought the model out there was Patti Smith, Tom Verlaine, Richard Hell . . .

The *lifestyle* of a poet was my ambition. (I say that in retrospect.) I was eighteen, nineteen. I was completely informed by Patti Smith, hanging out at the Gotham Book Mart. Yes, I was doing gigs at CBGBs. It was the beginning of punk rock and we were trying to create our own identity. I would see Ted Berrigan wandering around—I thought he was some hippy cult leader strolling around the East Village with young acolytes trailing him.

Now when I read somewhere it's the musician "writing poetry" and so not a "poet," I don't want to be that. I don't want to be an indie rock artist hanging his paintings in a gallery. But also at this point, I don't care. If I want to be a writer and write poetry, or write song lyrics, I do. In fact in 2015 I published a book called *Stereo Sanctity* which came out initially on my own imprint, Ecstatic Peace Library. One half was my complete song lyrics, and the other half poetry. And in it I wrote an essay about lyric and poetry writing emerging from the same source, and the different histories and how they co-relate.

THE INTERPLAY OF WORDS AND MUSIC

George Wallace: Talk to me about that—the relationship between writing song lyrics and writing poetry.

Thurston Moore: With lyrics the words can be dependent on the music to create some kind of unity. Whereas I find poetry on the page is singular in and of itself. With poetry you are much more aware of staying away from rhyme schemes—they can be hokey on the page but in a song they are integral. Rhyme is a point of delineation. Lyric writing has a freedom to it because it's supported by the music, whereas with poetry the music is implied both by the writer and the reader. That's a curious relationship for me, this distinction. Of course, when I write music I'm able to take poetry and re-jig it for lyrics. I may crib from poems to instigate lyrics.

I don't know when I write poetry itself, my music is in it at all. In fact, I don't write poems thinking about the way they sound out loud. For me it's more about how they read on the page. The eye, the brain. That's a different relationship. I can do readings and I enjoy them, but I'm not writing for poetry performance spaces, not at all.

When I first read "Howl" by Allen Ginsberg, there was a vocal ululation to it that I heard, right on the page. So when I heard Allen read it at St. Mark's Poetry Project, it was off-putting—it wasn't how I imagined it to sound.

LANGUAGE AND RHYTHM

George Wallace: Beyond lyrics versus poetry, I mean. You compose music, of course. What is there about the nature of music...rhythm, beat, sonority...that figures into your poems?

Thurston Moore: Clark Coolidge says language and rhythm have a pure and aligned moment of action. It's got humor and pathos and every emotional aspect of the human experience running in it, and it has music in it. I can completely relate to that. But to me, I'm attracted to other aspects of what Clark's doing, such as the history of language poetry which he is very aware of.

I'm interested in the writing of the words on the page, for example Bernadette Mayer and others. I look at trying to strip the emotional and confessional out of the lines and allow the lines to have their architecture and visual nature. I find that very alluring. Working with words on paper without losing the sense of the romantic, the confessional, or hyperbole of activism.

Amiri Baraka gave a lecture a few years ago, suggesting that poetry has to engage the people or else it's just "la-di-da." He was very dismissive of anything that was not socially activist. I had a lot of problems with that. It was interesting coming from somebody who had such a strong relationship with Frank O'Hara who wasn't so much the activist. Baraka's perspective comes from being in the trenches of so much warfare in society; he felt it was the utmost importance as a writer.

Am I trying to be a punk poet? Naw! But I think of using a punk aesthetic with writing. It's engrained in my work. I utilize that in my writing.

WRITING CONNECTIONS

George Wallace: Tell us about your association or collaborations with poets today.

Thurston Moore: I'd say I have something more like connections than collaborations. Writing connections. Like with Byron Coley . . . who you'll remember, George. He put on that Peace Ecstatique festival in Amherst, Massachusetts a few years back. I also collaborate in a journalistic way with Byron. He has a fanzine, *Bull Tongue*, taken from an Ed Sanders line. I sometimes write for that.

I do work a lot with Anne Waldman as I've been teaching at the summer writing workshop at the Jack Kerouac School of Disembodied Poetics at Naropa University in Boulder, Colorado. I'll do it again in 2016. It is only a week, not that intensive, but pretty interesting. It's not just Anne, but everybody who's there on faculty of that summer. In addition, I have recently done some collaborations with Clark Coolidge. I knew his poetry, certainly, but I was also aware of the fact that he was in a jazz-poetry psychedelic group called Serpent Power with David Meltzer and Tina Meltzer, his wife at the time. I'm a jazz aficionado, you see. So I have done some recording with him—Clark does free jazz drums, I do free improvisation music with him.

There's a book I want to do with Tom Clark and Clark Coolidge, based on their fascination with music writing and record reviewing. It's an unpublished manuscript titled *Rock Writing from the mid 70s*. Trying to figure out how to publish this! I'm involved in a small print called Flowers and Cream with Elaine Kahn. We've worked with Anselm Berrigan and John Coletti. It costs money to do this stuff. I do what I can.

When I write poetry I don't usually send it to anybody. I do remember writing back and forth with Larry Fagin for awhile. I was enamored, he sent me an invitation to collaborate with him. But then he sent them back with a few edits, not a lot of changes. Actually it turned out that he had this idea that I'd play the music, he would supply the poems.

CHANGING TECHNOLOGY

George Wallace: How do you deal with the changing nature of technology of your industry?

Thurston Moore: Audience does effect me and with today's audience I feel I need to be honest about my own history. In a way that means I'm trying to devise a way of dealing with the onslaught of technology. With new technologies of communication, there's always an obligation to respond.

Mostly I think about that in terms of the music world and how music is disseminated now. Because of the new economic structure, there's a tendency to trounce on years of sophisticated technology from the analog world. It's not the end of the world, but I have a certain responsibility to my own history as someone who teaches and shares.

It's kind of a new experience for people of a certain age. I'm fifty-seven. I feel like I need to step away from the technology of communication. I'm happy collecting books, archiving poetry books that are made by small publishers and poets. They're disappearing a lot from libraries—they're in private holdings if at all. I've spent years amassing this work.

In fact, I want to write a new manifesto . . . living off the grid . . . without getting too hysterical about it. I visited Gerald Melanga recently. He has this typewriter and he was writing an actual letter and putting it in an envelope.

That's not an old fogey, back in the day kind of thing. It's just basically a realization of the grace and simplicity that poverty has, as opposed to what you can do with more and more money, or objects equated to money.

THE SEARCH FOR PLACE

George Wallace: Actually every time we try to catch up with you, you seem to be off the grid somewhere. Emerging from some exceptionally compelling location and about to enter into a new one. Hiking the deep woods in France. Holed up in a beach house on Long Island. Engrossed in a rehearsal studio in New York or in London. Is there some hidden roadmap to all this?

Thurston Moore: A lot of it is happenstance, where I find myself. I let these things define themselves and accept the randomness of life's challenges. But I embrace these realities. What are the signifiers here, what are the activities there?

I have a fantasy of relocating to Paris, doing nothing except disappearing into some pied-a-terre and writing poetry, and not dealing with the mania of the society we have right now. I even ask my girlfriend, "Would you mind if I move to Boulder Colorado and do nothing but write poetry and study Buddhism?" The reality is that's not happening, but I'm still trying!

My reality is I look for where the poetry is. I have a sensitivity to not exploiting the profile I have as Sonic Youth but to just be in the common continuum of poetry and music.

THURSTON MOORE is a singer-songwriter, composer, poet, author and publisher. In 1976, at eighteen years of age, he moved to New York City and devoted himself to music and literature. In 1980, he founded and named the celebrated experimental rock band Sonic Youth, releasing their first album in 1981. Since 2011, Thurston has been on faculty at the summer writing program at The Jack Kerouac School of Disembodied Poetics at Naropa University in Boulder, Colorado —a school founded in 1974 by poets Anne Waldman and Allen Ginsberg in accordance with the Buddhist scholar Chogyam Trungpa Rinpoche. *Stereo Sanctity*, a personal selection of Thurston Moore's poems and lyrics, both with Sonic Youth and as a solo artist, written between 1981 and 2014 was published in 2015 in a limited edition from Ecstatic Peace Library.

Moscow, Russia

3 November 2015

THURSTON MOORE

Yesterday you pointed me
   to a gold ray of sun
      glowing the ancient paint
      of a woman's dress
       in the museum

Today you strode through the airplane
   clutching a handful of chocolate bars
     for me and our friends

Each of these times your smile
   was the perfect beauty of nature

They shut Red Square!!
   so people could wave flags
     and sing
  But the bookstore
     is open

   !!

I love you
   alone together
and within the buzz
   of our wild society

i.e.

KIT KENNEDY

Night is a place-
holder for the unsettled.

You, an eloquent verb
in another's mouth.

PB&J

SAVON BARTLEY

Peanut butter and jelly sandwiches
look like the cracks in Grannie's hands
caused by her memory lapses
which collapses the strawberry fabric of time
rapidly unraveling behind her.

Grannie forgot about me
but remembers the location of the church that she was raised in.
When I was young
I hated the days when I heard Grannie's affliction tell her to run away from home again.

And again
And again
And again.

Escaping from the family she now refers to as strangers.
We changed the locks on the door.
We were scared God would invite her to go live with him.

When I was a kid, she would shuffle her way into the kitchen.
Her feet made the sounds of
two brooms sweeping across sandpaper.

With wrinkled hands delicate as fallen petals off a hospital bouquet
Grannie taught me how to make a peanut butter and jelly sandwich.
It's been eight years since trembling hands cut diagonally across wheat bread.

The doctor said her brain was rotting.
A slow decay
like an ancient civilization.

Her skull is an elephant graveyard of her life recollections
only to have her life resurrected at the disease's convenience.

Names and faces became elusive.
The five children she gave life to never happened.
Grannie never said goodbye
to the cancer-prone sister dementia said she never had.

It's not just a sandwich.
It's a moment
when everything still made sense.

A moment before, Grannie started frantically grasping
at the thoughts she once thought belonged to her
as they were quickly auctioned off to the devil.

Retrospect became jelly.
The tighter she held
the quicker it oozes out of the palms of her mind.

I wish I could trap her memories in a jar of peanut butter
so they had a better chance at sticking.
Alzheimer's is a systematic annihilation of all the neurons in her brain.
My great-grandmother's smile makes genocide look so peaceful.

Out of love, we strangers do the things that she can't do for herself.
Bathe her in a tub
filled with tears of her daughters
praying they can wash the disease out of the creases of her skin.

Dress her in the love of the only son she says she never knew.
Spoon-feed her memories of holding her great-great-grandchildren.
After eighty-four years, Alzheimer's slipped her maturity up its sleeve.
Pulling off the greatest mind trick that I have ever witnessed

I would rather her just die.
Peanut butter and jelly
is the ability to relive the moment that we spent together
etched into forever.

We took the locks off the door.
We were hoping God would invite her to go live with him.
Whenever she's ready.

timing

ANNA HOLMQUIST

today at 3:22 am thursday morning the whole world has its finger
on my panic button so i have
ridden my bicycle alone to a park
and past your house and back again to my porch steps.

today at 3:23 am thursday morning the birds
are calling to me, which i hate because i have not gone to bed yet
and they are waking up—
or perhaps they think it is still day
in the mock twilight of chicago.
the street lamps here are bright enough to read a book by.

today at 3:24 am thursday morning i am counting
minutes with a fist in my belly
and clenching my jaw, and spinning my mind
until i don't know which way is up.

i used to believe 3:25
that i was strong but
each minute pulls me apart 3:26

and i don't know what to do other than sit in the cold and let it bite my fingers,
the pre-pre-dawn chill of early may in the midwest
and i am wishing i could see stars
because they always used to root me

3:27 and i don't know exactly what is wrong but it's been wrong all day
and i don't know if it will be tomorrow
but i would like to go to sleep.
i would always like to sleep but it is difficult
i have never been good at sleeping.

o chicago your arms are tight and your friends too familiar 3:28
i am setting limits and goals for myself and they are very easy.
breathe, make it to 3:30 breathe

breathe stop looking at the clock breathe 3:29
it is only one more minute breathe

o chicago at 3:29 on a thursday morning i have to work tomorrow
and i am in love and i am so alone like i have never felt before
the most empty hollow woman i have ever been

a chasm, 3:30

Extract from "Diary of My Body"

ZOÉ BESMOND DE SENNEVILLE

I am forgetting
Your face
Willingly
Thinking all the time about
The way you'll be earning your life
I am clearing up
Who am I gonna wait for then
What will we think of
Inside

But I need to be
Watched looked at cared
It is never the end of the story
That's the best of the best

Ah
By the way
I am here I am here I am here
I am in this very space with you

I have turned
My whole self
To one body
That even doesn't exist at all

Why are you going
So far in your aversions
In/On your diversions
In/On your tenderness
The crushes the clutches

Who are you who are you who are you who are you who are you who are you
who are you who are you who are you who are you who are you who are you who
are you who are you who are you who are you who are you who are you who are
you who are you who are you who are you who are you who are you who are you
who are you who are you who are you who are you who are you who are you who
are you who are you who are you who are you who are you who are you who are
you who are you who are you who are you who are you who are you who are you
who are you who are you who are you who are you who are you who are you who
are you who are you who are you who are you who are you who are you who are
you who are you who are you who are you who are you who are you who are you
who are you who are you who are you who are you who are you who are you who
are you who are you who are you who are you who are you who are you who are
you who are you who are you who are you who are you who are you who are you
who are you who are you who are you who are you who are you who are you who
are you who are you who are you who are you who are you who are you who are
you who are you who are you who are you who are you who are you who are you
who are you

who are you who are you who are you who are you
who are you who are you who are you who are you
who are you who are you who are you who are you
who are you who are you who are you who are you
who are you who are you who are you who are you

who are you
who are you
who are you
who are you
who are you
who are you

who are you

who are you
who are you

Normal: Adjective

LINDSY J. O'BRIEN

1. According with, constituting, or not deviating from a norm, rule, or principle.

2. Conforming to a type, standard, or regular pattern.

3. Synonyms: average, common, cut-and-dried, everyday, garden-variety, ordinary, prosaic, run-of-the-mill, standard-issue, unexceptional, unremarkable, workaday.

4. Examples of *normal* (in Smalltown, Minnesota *circa* 1990s—Disclaimer: All or most of these characteristics have been derived from the distant past of one particularly anxiety-prone Midwestern girl and refer only to her remembered ideas of what constitute the word *normal*):

    a. Fair-skinned people of primarily Scandinavian or Western European descent following one of several Christian denominations (Catholic, Lutheran, Baptist or the like).

    b. Such people seek out their identities within small towns that were built around 1860 on some form of industry, i.e. mining, railroads, or shipyards. The social lives of these towns include the corner gas station, high school football games, and the neon sign that flashes the name of the most recent All-Conference high school athletes.

    c. Typical childhoods are spent in two+ bedroom houses with one father and one mother. One or both parents may work outside the house. If one parent does not work, it is the mother (though she is responsible for all or most housework, cooking, and childcare either way).

    d. Family will attend church three or more times per month and will spend the skipped Sundays eating steak and potatoes and harboring guilt.

    e. One parent may struggle with various stages of alcoholism.

f. Father will spend time hunting, wearing wood-pulp-flecked work shirts, fixing his 70s era Mustang, and watching *Die Hard*. Mother will occupy herself with aforementioned housework, reading Nora Roberts romance novels and the occasional bit of literary fiction, hiding unnecessary purchases from the father (such as clothing, more expensive pre-cooked dinners, and school/extra-curricular expenses for the children), and speed-walking.

g. Holidays are accented with Jell-O salad prepared from Grandma's recipe by one of the few aunts on speaking terms with the rest of the family. Other holiday offerings include green bean casserole; a seasonally appropriate meat; and judgment, veiled with sarcasm, of various family members' life choices.

h. A *normal* condition for a firstborn daughter in such a household is an over-whelming sense of responsibility for every aspect of family and personal life. This anxiety manifests itself in perfectionism:

    i. "Perfectionism involves unrealistic levels of expectations, intangible goals (i.e. perfection), and a constant lack of satisfaction, irrespective of performance" (See: *The Corsini Encyclopedia of Psychology* by Irving B. Weiner, 2010).

        1. Thus, a type-A personality Midwestern girl will obsess over her inability to meet and exceed the expectations of others. She will eventually fall into a pit of burning panic-despair because of this, even though the standards she holds herself to are self-imposed, ambiguous, and ever-changing.

i. Another condition found in anxiety prone firstborn girls from this background is a belief that something *normal* exists in the rest of the world that the adult-child is incapable of achieving in her own life (See: *Adult Children of Alcoholics* by Janet Geringer Woititz 1990, Health Communications).

j. Normality, (also known as normalcy) is the state of being *normal*: when someone's behavior conforms to the most common behavior in society.

k. "Social norms define behavior as abnormal if the behavior deviates greatly from accepted social standards, values, or norms. Norms are unspoken rules for proper conduct" (See: *The Corsini Encyclopedia of Psychology*).

    i.   "For example if one was to witness a man jumping around, nude, on the streets, the man would be perceived as abnormal, as he has broken society's norms about wearing clothing, not to mention one's self dignity" (See: "Abnormality:" Wikipedia).

    ii.   Nobody wants to be the nude man jumping around on the street. Especially not an anxiety-prone type-A perfectionist firstborn female. The paralyzing fear of this will result in migraine and tension headaches, premature gray hair, arthritis, hyperventilation, numbness in hands and feet, acid reflux, vertigo, panic attacks, and an embarrassing case of IBS.

5. Heteronormativity, as a term, was likely coined in Michael Warner's 1991 article "Introduction: Fear of a Queer Planet." It has been defined as "the social and legal preference for heterosexuality and traditional [one man and one woman] marriage" (See: *Straight is Better: Why Law and Society May Justly Prefer Heterosexuality* by George W. Dent, Jr., 2011).

    a.   Heteronormativity suggests that anyone who deviates from the social norms of heterosexuality is *not normal*.

    b.   If, at age eleven, a small-town anxiety prone perfectionist entertains the possibility she might not be heterosexual, she will panic. In order to avoid a racing heart and waves of utter terror, this individual, at age thirteen, makes a vow that she will not break the societal norms of heteronormativity. She decides that, if she realizes that she might be homosexual at any time, she will instead be alone forever.

6. Antonyms for *normal*: abnormal, exceptional, extraordinary, odd, out-of-the-way, strange, unusual.

    a.   Rather than face the shame of being labeled *abnormal*, many people will choose to ignore aspects of their identity in order to conform to what society accepts as *normal*. Young people may tell themselves they are "normal until proven otherwise," and if they are logically minded, they will come up with a detailed list of arguments to prove that they truly are *normal*. These arguments (in the mind of a young female perfectionist) would include the following assumptions:

i. It is *normal* to be more attracted to women than men because women are more sexualized in the media, and any reference to sex can make people feel pangs of attraction.

ii. Obviously a young girl would feel more comfortable around women, so it makes sense that she would gravitate toward them in early adolescence and continue to do so into adulthood.

iii. Early experiences with sexual abuse by a family member (such as a teenage uncle) may make a young woman more uncomfortable around men.

iv. As noted above, a person is allegedly "*normal* until proven otherwise." Thus, if said person does not *know*, without a doubt, that she is homosexual, then she will assume that, deep down, she must be attracted to men.

b. By age eighteen, this young woman will manage to pathologically deny every bit of mounting evidence that she is not what she thinks she should be, to the point that she endures constant pangs of guilt that she is incapable of acknowledging.

c. She will date a list of guys with names like Matt, Jason, Frank, Mike, Al, Aaron, Eric, Nate, Matt, Rory, Nathan, Brian, Ryan, Scott, and Matt.

i. she will tell herself on the first date with each guy that the reason she is bored is because she isn't trying hard enough.

ii. On the second date when she doesn't want to let Matt-Jason-Mike-Ryan hug her goodnight, she will seek comfort in the idea that it is natural to not want to be touched by a person who is almost a stranger.

iii. On the third date when she sits side-by-side on the couch with Matt to watch *Million Dollar Baby*, she will shrink away from his body, straining her neck so that she ends up with a tension headache the next day.

iv. On the fourth date when he tries to kiss her, she will giggle, say goodnight, and begin the systematic process of "cutting him out" (screening his calls, taking 24+ hours to respond to his texts, and "forgetting" his email address).

      v.   She (and those who love her) assume that this behavior is just "pickiness." At the same time, she wonders why loving the appropriate gender seems to come so easily to everyone else.

     vi.   She will begin to believe she is irreversibly broken.

  d. In her mid twenties, this woman ordains herself online in order to perform the wedding ceremony for her younger sister. While prompting the blissful young couple to recite their vows, she realizes that her entire body is heavy with a sadness she can't explain.

  e. Denial of the self, coupled with the nearing of a milestone like a thirtieth birthday, will trigger extreme panic, depression, suicidal ideation, and putting together of collages while crying and listening to the soundtrack to the musical *RENT*.

  f. Would this be so difficult if the Type A Perfectionist had been born in New York or Los Angeles? She will suddenly start to wonder how much of what is abnormal is based on what is "normal" to a particular place or time or family.

7. And thus she wonders if, in order to change, she needs to create an entirely new life to exist within, a life that opens up the possibilities to what might be called "normal."

8. New Normal: "The current state of being after some dramatic change has transpired. What replaces the expected, usual, typical state after an event occurs. The new normal encourages one to deal with current situations rather than lamenting what could have been" (See: Urbandictionary.com).

  a. What becomes important from here on out is the anxious leap from 'a' to 'b'.

  b. Suddenly, what matters most is for this Type A Midwestern girl to get herself to accept the New Normal when it comes.

Husband and Wifey

GABRIELLA M. BELFIGLIO

Shmoogedy Shmoggedy
Gertrude and Alice B.
kept house with modesty
in Paris, France.

Never claimed (either one)
bisexuality.
Alice wore flowered hats,
neither wore pants.

Attached

EMMA WOOTTON

recently
people keep asking me about
babies
as if
my womb
is suddenly worth something
just
because
our relationship comes with a
penis already attached, so

      in response
i give them my
sexual history as if
sitting in clinic &
answering questions about
my previous lovers,
clinical & shameless
& waiting for the
judgement to come, just

          please do not assume that i am
          something i am not.

presenting as heteronormative unnerves me
in the way drinking too much coffee
makes me shake but
like the addiction it is i
keep on lapping us up,
navigating the art of being
both
the only way I can.

still, a girl i once knew told me to
write my poems muscled
& testosterone fuelled
hard on the page
because
who can differentiate these days anyway?
the world outside the bedroom
has its hands up in surrender to
gender & perhaps i've already
written enough about women &
roses & cunts &
you are without a doubt the
greatest
                              fuck
i've ever had

Universal Desperation

TSAURAH LITZKY

John Cheever is my favorite author. If I was as apathetic as I say I am, I wouldn't even have a favorite. This apathy I am cultivating is like a black leather motorcycle jacket. It would be boring if it was not so seductive and beautiful. If I was truly apathetic, if I didn't feel anything and had no expectations, my hopes wouldn't keep sinking lower and lower like the number of available, interesting (to me) men. My friend Ursula says, "How can you admire John Cheever? He is so last century, so passé, so far from what's happening. He writes about suburban housewives in Mt. Kisco or rich blue bloods on the Upper East Side. His women wear real fur coats that are not even second hand. Why can't you idolize someone interesting like David Foster Wallace?"

I tell her I love John Cheever because his characters live in the same state of universal desperation I do, both outstretched hands constantly stretching at straws.

I found out why that Damian didn't call me. His roommate sits down next to me at the bar about a week ago. Before he even orders a drink, he says, "I'm so pissed off at Damian. He moved his girlfriend into our loft and that wasn't part of the deal."

I pretend the top of my head hadn't just been blown off. Damian was telling me how lonely he is and how happy he is to meet me and all the time he has a girlfriend. Is he insane or is there something about me that turns men into compulsive liars? This is the third time in that many months something like this has happened. How anyone gets together is a mystery to me.

My mother tells me my standards are too high. I tell her that is a terrible thing to say to her own daughter. However, after Sean—who looks like Clint Eastwood—tells me he doesn't want a relationship with me because he heard Jewish women can never be trusted, I think there might be something to what my mother is saying. So a few nights ago at the bar, I allowed Anton—who was always wanting to chat me up—to buy me a drink. He was from Poland and had a continental manner, always bowing when he said hello and kissing my hand. He also weighed three times as much as I do. I couldn't imagine taking his weight on me but maybe I could always be the one on top, sliding gracefully up and down like a monkey on a greased pole.

He came to my show at the Bowery Poetry Club. Afterwards, he invited me out for a drink. We went to the Sidewalk Cafe. He brought me a double Absolut and told me I was very beautiful. He then unbuttoned his shirt to show me the angel he had tattooed around his left nipple. He said he had got the angel tattoo in the hopes love would fly into his heart. There was something about this gesture that touched me, the angel was so beautiful with big blue eyes. I told Anton I had just had a big disappointment in love, but if we took it very slow there might be hope for us.

He took my small hand in his two enormous ones and said, "Of course, of course, my darling. You have just made me so happy." He asked me to drop him off at his studio.

When I stopped the car in front of his door, he took my hand again. I thought he was going to kiss my hand again in his continental manner. Instead he jumped on top of me, pinning me behind the steering wheel, and thrust his huge tongue into my mouth. It smelled like herring. I tried to push him off but I wasn't strong enough. He wiggled his tongue around frantically and finally withdrew it. "Good night, my darling," he said and dashed out of the car.

The next day when he called, I told him everything was over between us.

"Why, why my darling?" he asked.

I said, "What about my wish to take it slow?"

"But I was taking it slow," he answered.

Last year I was writing a poem about Galileo because I was fascinated by his enormous scientific achievements. I read in Wikipedia that it took the Church 350 years to finally forgive Galileo for proving that the earth revolved around the sun. He had to say it was the other way around or get burned at the stake. He is supposed to have whispered as he rose from his knees, "E pur se muove" ("but it does move.") Even if he whispered, considering the consequences, he had the last word.

I can't compromise. If I was not such a chicken, I'd tattoo *No Surrender* around my left nipple. Maybe I will fall in love with a delivery boy from the supermarket like Melissa did in the John Cheever story. If Galileo didn't exist, John Cheever would have invented him. His characters are always looking up to the heavens in search of an epiphany and it was Galileo who made the first telescope.

When he looked through it, he saw how the surface of the moon—which, when looked at with the naked eye, appears to be so smooth and shining with reflected light—actually has a bumpy, lumpy surface. Sometimes I wonder about those happy couples, the ones I see walking on the street glowing with radiant light. I wonder if I just knew more about them, would I find their lives are like mine? As bumpy and lumpy as the surface of the moon?

the fly escapes the kitchen towel

MARCIA ARRIETA

typewriter the morning
eyes like art printed

manuscript the rabbit
caught in snow

Cornell & I conceptual

Beethoven

for Josh Radnor

WILL ARBERY

When I said I'd take fate by the throat, I was wrong. I'm getting old, and there is nothing I can do. But in my deterioration is a new thing, so clear, a note, a new thing every day. I faithfully record what sings singed under the new char and ash. When all this is over, I'll swim what I've done to an enormous sea warehouse and cast it all in. What floats, I wonder? And I will sit and hum and thank you. As it is, you have to be halved. Half craftsman, half crafted. Your art endeavors towards enigma, you can force your way into its secrets, you may feel perverse, you cannot tell anyone. Hold, hold. No. I am no longer the world-bitter mistress. I'm getting to hear them all in the sky! And then slowly again. Decaying. I'm so tired. I said: music is like a dream, and I cannot hear it. But now I know that you cannot hear me. What you hear is not me. What I am is a body. I came into the house, when I was nineteen years old, and the battle began immediately. It continued into the night. It took several days. We fought and fought and when I was through, we were both stronger and I ripped and I was new. Father, I flirted with your death and in the, oh, in the, oh, in the light from the bones . . . hold, hold . . .

I'm Praying for You!!!

LIV MAMMONE

Universe, God, Great
Clockmaker, Magician, Trickster,

Mother, Math Problem, make
their motives pure.

I can't because of that
thorn bush in my chest cavity.

Madison Square Garden (nothing growing here
but the hot ore of my ire)

make boomerangs of prayer and neon.
Put the pity back on these people—they need me so much

to make them good. Let the CO_2
in their *Jesus loves you!* be used

making a rose last a little longer
on its way to September. Send that belief

to a penguin's egg about to roll
off the edge of a cliff. Send it to the homeless boy

with the blue eyes and pair of pit bulls I saw on 57th;
the young and trembling vet just off Times Square;

the shaved-headed girl whose cardboard Sharpie psalm
proclaims her an incest survivor.

To the pulse of that shelter dog who'll be adopted tomorrow?
To Jack, so something can counteract the cigarettes? To Sandra Bland's family.

To an itchingly alive set of scars
from a top surgery. To Florence Welch's throat.

To Harper Lee. To Tara Hardy. To my first sister's serotonin
and my fourth sister's son. To the blind Romani woman I saw

sitting outside the Opera Garnier.
To a child, a soldier—to every child soldier.

To sex workers. To the forthcoming production
of *RENT*. To a student up late tonight practicing the cello.

To my sixth grade science teacher,
Mr. Otto, who had the first great ass

I ever noticed on a man. To every stop-motion
animator. Or can you expand the life of every salmon

(so there'll be more for me to eat?) Can I keep a coral reef alive
an hour longer? Could I be

the kinetic force that pushes her
through the rehab door? Can't

it go to every polar bear, or every elephant in mourning?
Emilie Autumn's violin, Amanda Palmer's stockings?

Could I ask red hair to grow on the heads of twenty babies? Could I be the force
that stops a blow? Could I hoard their prayers?

Save them up and cast them forward to unclench
amidst the smoke and ash

into the first peach
after the end of the world?

Between their pity and my hate,
just seems too many heartbeats gone to waste.

Laudanum for Jack-A-Roe

JAN STECKEL

The last of my eggs are trying to jump ship.
My left ovary wants to chew its way out.
A hot water bottle pressed to my belly,
I moan, beached on my Sleep Number® bed.

When I was three, the glowing space heater
told me stories. My trundle bed was a caravel.
My teddy bear protected me from pirates.
Pillows fish-wriggled between my thighs.

At thirty-five, I pitched my birth control pills
off the Golden Gate. Estrogenized sturgeon
big as manatees swam under San Quentin.
There were plenty of female fish in the sea.

At forty-five, that sinister ovary swelled,
its capsule stretched with the king tides.
The naval surgeon in the Emergency Room
gave me tincture of opium for the pain.

Let my eggs float free like fish-roe rafts
adrift in the salty swell. I lie in my seabed
of crushed pearls. Above my head,
a keel groans and sunlight wavers.

blue [belewe] moon

SHIRA DENTZ

1.

something I don't like about eating
is that then you can't eat again for a while. I love eating
strings of attachment warp woof cotton seed thyme?

trying to talk into a volcano hole,
I'd make space in my head where he wasn't, a 60s Volvo flying in the sky. when I didn't
play dead, he'd mirror albeit exaggerate my movements, that word *albeit* too grand a
misstep
imbues a dash of dignity and reason

trying to talk

everything swallowed everything
inside a capsule
mint-leaf
hill of an echo

in my everything-capsule that sky

2.

carousel voodoo
the way you do alphabet
hunk a hair Penelope brick an eye telepathy
want to stretch like a ballerina repeat sounds
movements
effortless
criss-cross antlers don't have a narrative

in a dream you said opposites of what you were doing

criss-cross antlers don't have a narrative
too bad no one to share this blue sky, particular cast of shadow, defined shapes of sun on
green.

3.

*

*

spell

tale carved inside a cave fanning out like a cockle shell: *cave* signifying *echo*. I could only
watch the strokings of marks being made, added to those already there, amassing like a
city or cities. even if the story isn't legible, recording had to happen

tracks—swirls, crags,
it's very important to know the tale circling

4.

* * *

Spinoza daddy long legs spins his top *// there's a limit to how much you can consume* oh that's why my food bill's so high when I buy all this summer fruit and some of it goes bad? trick is make lunch smell the herbs crunch a few, make tea, go to work, leave lunch on the table for later.

a blue moon's expected tonight;
last night's was fully full?

5.

* * * *

see-through acrylic cage by Price Chopper's exit:
about a ¼-filled with stuffed animals adults can buy for ᵗʰᵉⁱʳ/ₐ kid , dingy colors and shapes. what story would make these look good to a kid? maybe one who wants and wants and only wants to proclaim wanting because what they really want they don't get. then again, maybe I'm just not seeing this through a kid's eyes. what would it be like if I had a kid: would I view these animals differently?

blue moon gleams like a tooth
or is it glass   or ice?

last night's moon towered, eye to eye,
not letting me go.

tonight's though
most assertive I've seen. a period in the sky.
there's just nothing left to say O

6.

* * * * *

a voice can prickle skin.
often
I felt unfully dressed with my father; scantily; as if what I was wearing was partly sheer;
translucent. I wanted to cover up.
creepily because I was fully clothed and couldn't get any more so, what could I do to
close, resolve, the slippery limitless fractioning, feel full and thereby uncontaminated?
felt guilty for seedlings or whatever leaving me open. saw two spheres at once: as when
looking out a car window you see a landscape reflected at a different angle from the one
you see racing by squarely and head-on.

7.

* * * * * * *

on the sky outside Price Chopper a dark cloud like an animal skin rug. I see my car's red
runt, and a pregnant lady with a big belly walks by. I remember Montreal's giant distinct
clouds vaulting its sky.

summer mountains here: green, rounded, and still; uncratered or jagged like in the Southwest where light catches differently moment to moment.

I'd like to live somewhere quiet is velvet, though not solo.

8.

* * * * * * * * *

my mother would think it a kindness to be said of her:
her shell stayed intact unto her death.

her nothing an iron branding my kid-gut as if it were a shirt collar whose points needed flattening. a branding pause
  whose points
    needed flattening. a maternal nothing pause

this gulf

      a pause

in her 80s now, once in a blue moon she writes me;
today's ending salutation is "stay cool."

my stay whose *a* an *a* is, her a the her stayed will, will as to her shell, a pleading, call, gulf not said maternal my not in will not ended, her ended. I branding nothing. now intact points like a thing is, her hill, death. her about cool." intact could last flattening. being my gut on being pleading,

her collar a hill her never flattening
needed like nothing.

sky still a shade of blue. after sunset, *watch things grow indistinguishable from their background*. gradations of light dissolve, an insect chorus pulses multiplies like a congregation of stars O brightening and fading
O O all in relation—   perceiving one leads to perceiving an other

* * * * * * * * *

9.

for some reason, oddly, it's repeated this summer that as I'm walking through a supermarket parking lot that I'm about to enter or leave, I feel the day's beautiful, absolutely gorgeous, as if I'm at the beach or sailing. I can't wait to get home, sit outside & fully experience. when I return home, it's muggy and close. why this feeling of expansiveness in a supermarket parking lot? I'd like an answer to this riddle.

there's a limit to how much you can consume

10.

* * * * * * * * * *

today's shade of sky. as in the photo session for my brother's (now fully grown) baby pictures: three of us—my brother sick and who will die soon, our healthy baby brother, and me—all of us wearing this particular shade of sky.

*
*
*
*
*
*
*
*
*

collage sky now, weather shifting and simultaneously blue, white, and gray hues, dim as the early yellow of sunrise or pre-dawn—the color of newness, fragility with something heavy that makes one queasy, like loss. on the cusp $^{of}/_{between}$ life and death. now gold spots on leaves.

How to Detonate a Landmine

Inspired by the novel Absalom Absalom *by William Faulkner*

KHADJIAH JOHNSON

The first time I had my hand on a slave   I felt their sovereignty collapse   Their crowns colliding with the praise dance of my slave ship.   I came from a lower class   "white privilege"   You understand, right? To have a body   people crave to   but refuse to accept the negative connotations that come with it?
Example, I step outside
Sun wreaks havoc against my pigmentation,
I transform from white cheddar
To a bruised alabaster

Yet when a murky-skinned concubine   Peeks out of from the shadows   Concubine absorbs light   Melanin converts to Onyx   Don't you see why we whip you?   Attempting to find ourselves beneath all that obsidian?   The pink continuously ravishing against leather?   Isn't this what you wanted?

Nigger?
To become as bright as your lighter counterpart   To be accepted as house labor, rather than sugarcane-cutting captive

Look at how we took the magic   of dreadlocks and cornrows   then mask it as an artistic interpretation of slave grounds?
Don't you understand why the lack of white substance gives them withdrawals? Their

convulsions mimic the dance of whips crying against their backs. If you listen closely
their bones snap crackle and pop on beat, just like their ancestors.
Look how we rob your womb
Put a price on your son before he's cut from the umbilical cord.
We baptize you in this oppression
In the name of the slave holder, the whip, and the Negro spirituals.

Do you taste your kingdom now, slowly growing inside of cages? Isn't this the justice
you were looking for? A place to stay   during the ethnic cleansing,   as we feed it to
you as a
God
Complex? Isn't that what love is? Keeping you locked up; as you hopelessly die singing
hymns to a God we painted to look like us? Recognize the story? We've fed this to you
for centuries.
Innocent man, pierced body, weeping mother forced to bury her child
Haven't you realized your savior has gone through the same death your sons have been
trying to avoid for years?
And you still believe that your enslaved heavenly father which art in heaven
is white?

Politics

m.nicole.r.wildhood

we live in the days where peace is bread / and bread is wheatfield war / we can't do much besides / maybe survive them / them and then the shrieking lack of / but whenever you name it / it's not it even here under the bemused mornings / the slog to fit in or fill in or fill it / with all the soil something had to fall / to meet the light whose legs we are getting tousled in / our ways to work / and whose face so complete it could be music / we might never see / climb climb / they tell you and you'll see it and all / your birthrights but where are those / who it still feels wrong for / to translate another's labor into kingdom

Black Transience

A Monologue
by
CORNELIUS FORTUNE

Character
A man in his early or mid-30s in a waiting room.

Man: I hate the smell of waiting rooms.

I think it's the magazines, or the people. We're all in this existential crisis of waiting . . . for something. *(Pause.)* Locked inside our minds, dusty cramped places with collections of filing cabinets numerically categorized, and catalogued, by trauma.

Trauma level #1: Birth. No one remembers that, but it's tucked away in the subconscious, blanketed by the layers of human conditioning.

Trauma level #2: Also known as "getting to know *you*." Or dog trainers call it socializing. You must be *socialized*. Society thrusts you into its cavernous embrace and says, "adopt," "adapt," "replicate," "belong," but you've got to fit perfectly or find some other hell to fit, lodge in . . . hello, high school freshman year.

Trauma level #3: Love. Okay. It's our idea of love that's the problem. Love can't be crammed into a three-act structure with a happy ending straight ahead, just watch the curb, use your turn signal. Love has no structure. No shape to speak of. We're always trying to hold it in our hands, but its incorporeal nature eludes us, a vapor produced by our minds.

Trauma level #4: Any type of failure in adult life. Failure to get into the college you want. Failure to get a promotion. Failure to get the job you want despite having a degree that was supposed to make you marketable. Failure to lose weight. Failure to gain weight. Failure to read your partner's mind at any given moment appropriate to the situation. Failure to express empathy. Failure to say "I'm sorry." Failure as a parent. As a husband, wife, son, daughter, legal guardian, lover, best friend. Failure to stop at a red light. Which brings us to trauma level number five.

Trauma level #5: Traffic stops.

Let me pause a moment.

Traffic stops are usually the fault of the driver. Maybe you overlooked the no-turn-on-red-sign. Maybe you mistimed going under the amber light. Maybe you thought it was a good idea to drive 70 miles per hour in a 55 miles per hour zone. Maybe you forgot to have your brake lights fixed.

Most cases, driver's fault. But being black in America means that a simple traffic stop has a different meaning for you than your white counterparts. A traffic stop for a black man is a complex web of scenarios in which the outcome is uncertain.

Call it, "Being Black in America." It should be a handbook published by a major book publisher. It'll be a *New York Times* best seller. "Being Black in America" has usually taken the form of oral tradition, a set of rules, do's and do not's, passed down, generation to generation. The companion volume, "Being a Black Man in America," is much heavier —much heavier in a metaphysical sense—and by sheer volume.

It should be required reading.

It's like a Harry Potter novel, only in this case, we don't know if the boy lives at the end.

Ever try free-associating?

Let's try it.

(Takes a magazine, pantomimes going through the list point by point.)

Being Black in America means . . . *putting on black face from time to time—just to survive.*

Being Black in America is . . . *hard work.*

Being Black in America was . . . *safer from a skewed point of view.*

Being Black in America in the second decade of the 21st century . . . *is transient.*

Being a black man in America means . . . *you're a moving target that should not move, or think. Or breathe. You're Ralph Ellison's Invisible Man, a personified abstraction lifted off the page.*

Every traffic stop is a potential time bomb waiting to go off: either you, or the officer. Either or. Greater than, less than. Try to solve that equation.

"Do you know why I pulled you over?"

If you're black, that's one of the most chilling questions you'll ever routinely be asked.

I have no way of knowing yet how *my* brother answered that question.

I get a text from my sister, "Daniel's been hurt."

My first response was "Ice hockey again?"

(My brother's a brother that loves the ice, man.)

My sister sent two separate messages: "A cop."

"Pulled him over."

Let me tell you about my brother Dan. Dan created experiments in school using the Periodic Table of Elements as a guide. Dan was a straight 'A' student. Dan went to Princeton to pursue a degree in philosophy. He's a professor at a private university. Dan collects comic books and can tell you the first appearance of the original Flash in DC Comics.

Dan should have been given a ticket and sent on his way. But Dan's in an operating room fighting for his life.

My sister's stuck in traffic. And I'm stuck in this waiting room.

Socrates once said that "the unexamined life is not worth living."

Let's examine my life.

I pay taxes. I own a business. I'm divorced with no kids. My ex-wife and I get together on Christmas day and exchange gifts.

Remember the lady who was shot asking for help in a suburb of Detroit? That was literally five blocks from my house. You watch these things on TV all the time, and then it comes right to your backyard. North, south, east or west. The new racism finds you, wherever you lay your hat, or your heart.

One of the most complex riddles of life? Electing a black president was supposed to launch us into the parallel universe we call a *post-racial society*. In this parallel universe with flying jet packs, FTL travel, and universal translators like they have in *Star Trek*, we're a cohesive society without a wrinkle, our *ugly side* cosmetically lifted. We got drunk on the elixir of King's Dream taking shape right before our eyes, and then, gradually, the future tipped.

I tried something on my iPhone. You can try it too.

I said: "Siri, do you think that black lives matter?"

She says: "I'm sorry [insert name], I'm afraid I can't answer that."

And neither can we.

Listen, there was a time when I loved the confederate flag the same as everyone else. *(Pause.)* Don't act like you don't know what I'm talking about. I owned a General Lee car, and whenever "The Dukes of Hazzard" would come on, I'd park my General Lee right in front of the TV. Do the whole slow motion bit. I didn't see anything wrong with it, and strangely, neither did my parents. Boss Hogg was funny. He usually got his comeuppance.

But I've come to realize that white southern pride has a different shape than black southern pride. This is by design.

But when you're black, you're always stuck in a waiting room. You're always waiting.

You're waiting for things to get better or worse. You're waiting in an isolated room, a prison, a box, that's difficult to break free of. I thought my brother had broken free. I thought he was immune, but the disease caught hold of him.

If someone like him isn't exempt, then what room does that leave for me? Or any of us?

The doctor's coming out now.

It's your turn to wait.

On Living without Orchids

CAROL BROWN

I watch as he strides, long legged
lean, towards the bathroom door.
His naked buttocks bounce
    blossoming
        wilting
    blossoming
        again.
I marvel at the supple bend of him
how flower petal his soft sweet skin
how easy it tears when touched
too hard, new leaf bent in thunderstorm.

It is not that I didn't already
know this, the graceful way his body
flowers. I have seen this before.
He, orchid, has been growing inside
me for months now. His petals tickle
my esophagus in the faintest breeze,
but he blossoms differently at
a distance. I am enraptured by this.

The door closes. I am alone. The spell
breaks. My hands find the clean skin
of my thighs, the soft flower
hidden there—his delicate kin
in this, my flint and tinder body.

I touch
        touch and touch
        touch and touch
and touch until my body forgets
him orchid man to become instead
a constellation of stars, mighty
Ursa Major with her thousand fires,
burning through space
                        pulsing
                                magnanimously.

It is not that he hasn't already done
this—he has. He has fed this fire-brand
body good tinder and stoked her.
Simply, I burn different alone, hotter,
faster without the spring damp of a beautiful
orchid man. I know this, but today, my body
needs reminding, how beautifully I can
ache, how graceful my own good hands.
Today, I need to tear up roots, to rip the
orchid in my gut up out through my mouth.
This is how I perform my own surgery.
In this act, I am my own breaking
and my own repair—

        a reminder, how little I need that vase
        shattered on the floor, how easily I can
        sweep it away, forget it was ever here

                a reminder, how smoothly life continues through
                winter, not an orchid in sight.

For Her, Christ Has Become a Peacock

KATHARYN HOWD MACHAN

banging his chest against another male
on a palm-swung tin roof at Big Pine Key
a short drive down a single highway
to where our country America ends

she sends messages: *Make sure*
the pedestal is tall and strong, make
sure there's plenty of room for his tail
in the room where my long marriage ends

the man who stuffs birds is Christian, too—
his t-shirt spells out F–A–I–T–H—
and he looks back to an older world
where dangerous beasts met dreadful ends

Registry

PHILLIP STERLING

Her dishes were mismatched to begin with. Some of her set was porcelain, morning glories vining around the edge; some of it was Corelle. Several china teacups with matching saucers had been hand-painted with what looked to be pink lady slippers. One stoneware serving bowl boasted a bright sunflower. Most of the set had come from yard and rummage sales, the annual white elephant event at the church, estate auctions, curio boutiques, or consignment stores. She had collected randomly at first, what her whimsy begged, or what struck her fancy, which was, at the onset—as she herself admits—somewhat scattershot ("scatterbrained" was one lover's parting word), an aesthetic formed at a moment's spur and feint, at times reactionary even, given one's companion's pigheadedness. Yet over time her tastes solidified and she found herself with dinner plates or soup bowls of a distinctly yellowish-brown nature, though various tints of olive or mustard were tolerated as long as flowers were prominent, for flowers were essential to her collection. At Thanksgiving, her table looked like an overgrown English garden.

His dishes were mismatched to begin with. He had acquired them from his mother, her old dishes, dishes she was no longer happy with, or sets that were incomplete, with only three salad plates, for example, and a hideous blue and orange casserole dish someone had abandoned at a cub scout potluck. His mother had furnished him with dishes she had meant to drop at the Salvation Army years before but had misplaced; she found the box in a closet of the spare room, behind the cedar chest, when she was looking for bedding to send with him to college. During college, as he migrated from dorm to living space to apartment, he lost some of the dishes his mother had given him, lost or broke them (more than half of the glassware, in fact) and so replaced it periodically—at times with the white stoneware he filched from the dining hall, at times with the embossed china of some fancy eating establishment (taken on a dare). At the end, his collection included nine salt shakers, seven for pepper (though one, from the looks of the holes, may have been misused), two cheese mills, and a creamer.

The first time she stayed at his place (she would say, whenever someone asked), she had looked in his cupboard for a teacup and found a Goodwill Store. She had laughed. It was something they seemed to have in common. They both laughed.

Now they were talking marriage, or at least moving in together, simplifying, downsizing, combining the households (their fortunes and misfortunes), partnering.

"What do we do about the dishes?" she asked. "I mean, what will it say about us if we pack them up and give them away—return them to Goodwill or something, sell them in the yard? What will it say about us if we register at Macy's for a complete, matching set?"

"Or use them for skeet shooting," the man said, thinking less of his white plates than of her flowery brown ones, brownish birds winging across a pale blue sky. After all, his set was an heirloom of sorts; they'd been with him for years. They held certain memories. He couldn't bring himself to think of smashing them intentionally. Or giving them to strangers. Perhaps his sister's kids, his nieces, now that they approached their teens, would want his dishes, would pack them off to college, add to the collection, start a tradition, make of the dishes a family story.

"Or perhaps," she said, "we could salvage the ones we have the most matches to, the most complete set, add to it from open stock." She was thinking of the porcelain with the morning glories. Hadn't she seen something like that . . . or close enough . . . at Target?

"What's wrong with what we have already?" he said. "It seems silly to spend money on something we don't really need, at least not right away."

He spoke softly, from across the small table, where he sat on a chair that matched the one she was sitting on, though without the floral cushion. He didn't look up from the houseware catalog that overlapped the plate he'd pushed aside. His coffee mug prevented the page from turning.

"Want anything else?" she asked, rising. She hesitated, briefly, as if she had something more to say, then picked up the saucer she'd used for her egg and set it on the counter. A bit of yolk had already dried on the pattern, like a late yellow bloom caught in early frost. From where she stood, she could see through the window the neighbor's yard, their above-ground pool, which they had used maybe a half dozen times all summer. It was covered in a black tarp.

"No," he said. "Thanks."

It was October, a Sunday. And while the woman at the sink knew there were things that needed to be done—dishes to wash and put away, a skirt and blouse to set out for the morning, a thank-you note to send to her mother (important things, necessary things)—she could not move. Water from the faucet filled the sink, dumbing its clamor of mismatched dishes. The neighbor's pool looked pathetic. And the old sadness came back to her, familiar and fathomless.

Genderhood

VICKI IORIO

I got my period at 9. What the fuck? If only I had that word then. My mother would not let me go swimming, like the water would suck the blood out of me.

I hate wearing a bra. At the end of the day, I undo the hooks in excitement equal to ripped-bodice sex, lay down on my bed, take my first deep breath and drink it in like an aged single malt Scotch.

I was the scientist of my own pregnancy. Measured my linea nigre from pubic to fundus, weighed my exploding veiny breasts, treated motherhood like a bottle-fed business.

Who wants to be a woman at 9? Who wants to be a woman?

Used Bottles

GAYLE RICHARDSON

Not all women emotionally attach after sex.

I won't.

My notches are vodka bottles with faces
not individual waves
just sea
no snowflakes
just snow.

When I look at my list of scorned lovers
it becomes obvious I speak lover very well.

I talk sexy to every cocktail hour
screaming orgasm
sex on the beach
my vagina wetter than a virgin martini
craving ballsy pistols
shooting black Russian.

My notches are vodka bottles with faces
not hand-picked flowers
just gardens
no flames
just fire.

For every claw hack on the bedpost
I clap and laugh
blow the next better
expect nothing more
than the former
money shot.

I don't believe in finding superheroes
so swap your comic for a strip
barfly dance
raise your glass
this piss artist is dehydrated.

My notches are vodka bottles with faces
not woolly jumpers
just sheep
no poems
just words.

Stop expecting it to look like what you thought
I'm not that kind of tipple
instead
name me
whiskey
rum
gin
long island ice tea
manhattan
fool's gold
the love monkey
the punch bowl
as I openly swallow

we are all used bottles

half full
half empty

just waiting
for someone else
to top us up.

Penny Tragedies

SUE HYON BAE

...a case study that, we believe, scholars, policymakers, and regulators will want to study and debate for some time. For that matter, so might novelists, psychologists, and—if only they were still around—ancient Greek tragedians.

– "The Siege of Herbalife" by Roger Parloff, *Fortune*

Arthur Miller wanted to write a tragedy starring an everyman,
and so he did, and so Willy Loman is tragic,

and so is Miller's wife Marilyn who
didn't like how they all thought she was marrying

above her intellectual weight, and so is Joe DiMaggio,
who stepped up to organize his ex-wife's funeral,

and so is the way he used to abuse her, tempting
to separate him into old Joe and better Joe

but we must not, so is every frame of unused footage,
so are dogs in love with children who are frightened of them,

so is the Saturday morning in October when I stood alone
with brown Mississippi water crawling at my back,

so is Tennessee Williams' grave, because it is permanent proof
that they wouldn't let him follow Hart Crane into the sea, and also

my cousin's dead grandfather's favorite shade of lipstick,
every finger that flips hair onto a bald spot,

and every time a brand-new astronomer discovers that the dome
of the Harvard observatory opens up into a rectangle instead of

two petals unfolding to a round pool of stars with the moon smack in the center
—attention must be paid! That square sky broke my heart.

In fact, here is the only non-tragic detail so far:
when Hart Crane's drunk and bruised body hit

the Gulf of Mexico, there was an orchestral shout,
like the full cannon version of the 1812 Overture

condensed into a splash.

ashamed of myself

PTR KOZLOWSKI

When I first learned to be ashamed,
I learned to be ashamed of myself
because that's the way they put it,
not ashamed of something I did cause if they did
I might remember what it was but as it is
it's my self that bears the shame.
a lesson too easy and learned too well.
And I shrivel down in my shame
and I shrink down to the ground
feeling down because they put me down. And,
I like the ants.
The ants can just go about their business
like we're not in trouble;
they're not ashamed.
I like the ground. I like the dirt.
The grass is nice and soft, the clover so gentle.
And the topsoil smells delectable with life.
I like the worms. They can just go down in their little holes
and be safe from the looming humans scolding with their scorn
and with shame.
I envy the field mice and ground squirrels and moles.
They've got whole other worlds down there.
Lower than me. Lower than low.
And they don't seem ashamed.

So I got a shovel and I started to dig.
I wanted to make an underground playhouse.
We were living on a coastal plain then, not far from the creek.
You dig a certain ways down, a couple of feet or so,
you reach the dirt that isn't brown, it's yellow.
We called it China dirt. Like I was digging my way to China
and was starting to get there.
I wanted to go.
Yeah, I knew it was way too far but I wondered,
if you keep digging deeper, will there be other colors?
And if you could dig all the way through
there'd be a point somewhere about halfway
where down is not down any more.
Where down from where I was
becomes up to someplace else.
What happens to the shame
when you go down past the rabbit holes and below the aquifer?
Does it get burned off when you pass through the molten core?
Do the vicious circles all become virtuous ones,
as the water in the drainpipes starts to swirl the other way?
If I really could go down-becomes-up
to the other side of the world, I would
crawl up from the different dirt, and be under a different sky.
And be free enough to realize
that in space—every which way is up!
I'm a quantum entanglement / I'm a relativistic anomaly /
I'm the blossom of life on earth's resplendent diversity.
Maybe sometimes I'm a particle, and other times more like a wave,
and if you try to measure my mass, you
won't get the chance to clock my speed.
Because I'm an Event Horizon.

I'm a Prime Number of complications.
I'm a natural variation of evolving proliferation,
remembering shame,
where every which way is down;
inhabiting space, where every which way is up.

(Definitions of) Fun

TODD ROBINSON

1. If you piled all your coins on my belly, we could have some fun. 2. Please let's not drive past another feedlot. That kingly cow on the hillock does impress, though, shit dribbling from under his tail like who cares. 3. One time I saw a neighbor and his daughter walking and they hid from me behind a tree. I laughed at them, though not with every part of myself. 4. Last week, looking for beads to put in a piñata, I came across a bottle of vodka, heat trapped in glass. I thought who could I give this to? I was sober 360 days, a full circle of recovery, but that potato sweat seemed too sweet to waste. 5. Then I went looking for clay, and found a ball of hash. I remembered the times I had carved shavings and burned them on hot knives, but I threw it away. Forgive me, seekers. 6. We are born so cold, but strangers swaddle us, wipe the goo from our mouths so we can breathe. 7. My friend Kelli calls me weekly, but I never answer, though I am often lonely. She is beautiful, but we have never kissed. Her mother once dated a helicopter pilot. 8. My mother once dated a chef who refused to leave his ex-wife. I feel sorry for all of them. 9. My father's final girlfriend died of brain cancer five years ago. Suzanne, you resembled Billie Jean King, which made no sense. Dads prefer blondes.

10. Another time my girl and I were walking under tree shadows, a little high maybe, and this couple crawled out of an argument, roaring down the street. We crouched behind a car to listen. "Don't touch me," she said. "I will smash your fucking face." We tittered, happy it wasn't us, for once. She was blonde as ice. He was a generic man, face rubbery with booze. Then they spotted us. "Excuse me," she smiled. "We're just being vicious."

Resurrection Day

JOE BAUMANN

On Resurrection Day, we all huddle around the tiny black-and-white television in the kitchen clutching our tickets, one each. They are laminated and smooth, the barcode at the bottom and the thick, rigid numbers little humps you can feel if you slide your thumb over with a deft, light touch. We've all been holding them and staring at them for weeks, ever since the lottery opened, so that we certainly have them memorized. My number is 1092756324.

It used to be that they would draw one hundred numbers. Right when the technology was fresh, and people clamored for the chance to see a loved one reborn, there was a mad dash to shell out all the cash one could in order to scoop up as many tickets as possible. This was in the days of the two-hour lead-in special, when a camera crew and reporter would knock on random houses and ask the residents for their stories of loss and grief and just what it would mean to see a father, mother, sister, son, or whoever again. The specials were filled with touching piano music: threadbare major chords that swelled whenever the interviewee inevitably started crying. The people interviewed were always poor or lower-middle class, their houses all beige siding and wimpy thin columns with chipped white paint holding up sagging roofs in need of new shingles. The women wore thick glasses, hair frizzy, and the men sported bushy mustaches and day-old beards. Those pre-event specials didn't last, especially because every year at least one of the families would have a winning ticket and people started calling foul, claiming that the whole thing was rigged, and, as a result, people started buying fewer tickets.

Because of the dip in interest, the number of resurrections started to drop. First it was slashed to fifty, then twenty-five, and now a measly ten. Only ten people in the whole big, overstuffed, smoggy world would be chosen! The first time they cut the number of resurrections there were headlines and endless comments on the web about it, people clamoring for the CEO of ResAssure's head on a stick. The shift to twenty-five caused aches and groans and anger, but it was the final drop down to ten that caused near-riots, angrier op-ed columns verging on actual threats, and screaming television commentators that grew red in the face making impassioned cries over the injustice of it all. The CEO went into hiding, and his subordinates hired round-the-clock security. Police officers had to set up blockades at their HQ to deal with the protesters.

Then, of course, came the ethical questions. Not about the resurrections—no, no one seemed concerned about the rights of the dead, about whether those brought back would want to be alive again, even for only a few months before their bodies gave out, their reinvigorated cells losing their energy like a wind-up monkey, the kind who clashes cymbals together, running out of vigor mid-crash, his cymbals hovering an inch apart for all of eternity like two communion wafers staring at one another. No, the concern was fairness; the rich could afford many more of the one-hundred dollar tickets, buying them by the tens of thousands, the millions in a few desperate cases, leaving the rest of the world to grasp at their single slips of slick paper and hope to beat the odds.

Things have calmed down since all that, acceptance tamping down the flame of momentary rage and violence, and here we are: Mom and Dad and me and Jill and Grandpa in a tight half-circle at the kitchen table. It's kind of our parents to give tickets to me and Jill, but I know Mom and Dad expect us to swap with them if one of our numbers is ever called. Mom misses her sister Nancy, and she'd be an okay pick because she always bought me loads of bubble gum, the expensive, genetically engineered kind that never loses flavor or gets stiff like the other, cheaper stuff. I know Dad would choose to see his own father; Grandpa might choose Grandma. It's been six years since she died and he still carries a crinkly picture of her in his breast pocket. The photograph is large, because his vision is going cloudy and he wants to see her as clear as possible, he says, so there's a crease across her neck where he folds it, the paper white there from the friction, so it's like she's wearing a pearl necklace. He takes the photo out at all sorts of random times, stopping in the middle of the hallway or the grocery store or on the way out of church, freezing as if struck to stone, and then, after a moment, he'll reach into his breast pocket and pluck out the picture, unfurling it like a diploma.

Jill and I have whispered about who we would choose: she'd want to see her first-ever boyfriend Toby again, even though they only dated for a week before he was hit by a taxi driver while crossing the street at dusk. I told her that I would pick Butterscotch, my pet rat, and this made her crinkle her nose.

"No one ever picks an animal," she said, breathing raspy like she smelled sewage. "I don't think they can even do that."

"They can do anything. They're ResAssure."

I had never told anyone else who my choice was, even though it was the only thing anyone ever asked. I shrugged, and I always got a sideways look like, *of course you know the answer*. Everyone has an answer. Everyone thinks about who they would like back. For everyone alive, there is someone gone.

The announcer is a thin man with a wide middle, like a stick figure who's swallowed a watermelon. His slicked-back hair shines under a bright light, and he sits at a high, glassy desk. He has a face that is immediately forgettable once it is not in front of you but you remember with sharp certainty when you see it: of course, it's the same announcer. It is as if he only exists this one day out of the year but keeps returning. Costume makeup blurs the wrinkles of his cheeks.

Beside him, a massive tank full of papers: over two billion tickets this year, he says, filling his voice with wonderment, even though everyone knows this is less than a third the number from just a few years ago.

Outside, the sky turns gray; it always rains on Resurrection Day. The wind will pick up soon, just as the announcer slides toward the tank of tickets and reaches a hand in, giving it a good stir. He will stand up then, really reach down deep into the clear box, fingers stretched and pulsing, flitting over those slick little sheets with their bumpy digits and lines. With a smile he will stop suddenly, a ticket in his grip, and pull it out. A deep breath, and then the announcement, the numbers sliding out like kisses. Before the last number in the sequence, when ten people know they are so close to getting what they want, seeing a lost loved one, he will pause, smile up at the camera, and stare at every one of us, knowing that somewhere, staring back, is someone whose dream he will make come true.

Poem Where Mama Teaches Me to Twerk

WILLY PALOMO

My mama gotta big ol' nose, beak
like a hungry pajaro. Teeth like a mule-
kicked piano, as broken as her English.
In pictures, she chooses not to smile

con dientes—unless we make her
laugh & Mama's laughter can make
machetes look dull, the way it guts
a house of silence with its silver cut.

Yeah, Mama ain't much, but she got back.
Latin women, tu sabe, the way they carry
the world tumbao. The way men & gringos
look & think about you when they see

a fat brown ass. The weight of it, cracking,
its lovely slit & snare. The bass drum
it pounds in the muscles. This is not a song
where you can sit down & bop your head.

This that sweat as a child in fields of sugar
cane & cotton. This that slash coins made
in her pockets, selling tamales on the street
with no place to sleep. This the man cornering

her as she folds his wife's laundry. This him
gripping her ass. This *her ¡no! ¡puedo ser indita,*
pero no soy tu estupida! This the broken teeth
of her knife trembling inches from his face.

This is his laughter & fast hands. His threat
to slit her throat & rape her in the ass. His chase.
His boot, kicking a dent into the thin metal door
while she's trapped in his daughter's room.

This is patience. Faith. The three hours it takes
for him to give up, get drunk. This is her escape
to another family. Another country. Her song
ten thousand steps across a desert. When I say

I got my mama's ass I mean this: I'd come home
past midnight to find Mama's back bent
over, mopping the floor, cooking pupusas,
after her double shift & at the same time.

I mean, once I spent a summer day cleaning
the house top-to-bottom & when Mama came
home, she made me mop the ceiling. I mean,
once a white woman asked how Mama got that ass

& Mama passed her the vacuum. I mean,
I have never had to work a day of my life
as hard as my mama. Mama can't dance,
but the way she rocks it taught me to hustle,

surrender myself to the break,

twerk.

The Waters Recede, the Gates Consumed with Fire*

AJ URQUIDI

---

* Footprint drizzle[0] of a previous hiker
            prehistoric to the touch, crusted
    over edges: the crater of a minor
       meteorite, preemptive messenger[1]

long departed. A snipped filmstrip[2]
          sips the shoe's puddle, skitters
    over edges: on four billion needles
       housed in sable casing, with paired[4]

[3]

longitudinal yellow emanations.[5]
        It knits its monochrome tapestries
   of subaltern history[6] blurring silt edges:
      sea-ridge echo knee-deep in Carmel Valley.[7]

---

[0] Damaged landscape
    three thousand feet
       Jeep Trail devoured
          December downpour[i]
            blue-green flannel shirt
               suspenders, antler-bearded[ii]

[1] His ears open to the praying servant,[iii] exhuming the form of a poisoned child[iv]
[2] *Blood of the Beasts,*
      1950.[v] Also, a coastal
         California millipede.
[3] The white space[vi]
      from Jeep Trail
         mountain to Scenic
            Trail bluff measured
               three thousand feet
                  one thousand anapests
                    fiber-optic cable
[4] Two together, rift between, murdering brother-victim,[vii] genetic rivals conjoined at the eye
[5] Spirits, stripes. Strife
      or spears, spurious
         streets bisecting spelunca.[viii]
[6] *Speak for yourself v. "The God of heaven,*
      he will prosper us; therefore we
         his servants will arise and build" 1991.[ix]
[7] Treasure map
      subterranean trunk[x]
         Sierra Lode Trail
            forty paces west
               six-mile mark[xi]
                  Robinson Canyon Road

---

[i] We sped past McDonald's that night
while lightning struck the road ahead.
The children feared the car would
turn conductor, but Mother drove
on calmly into the thundercloud,
through death-crackle, safely home.

ii   A burly fellow with Polynesian
walking stick, I've seen his golf cart
before—by the lake in midsummer.
He waves hello with a soft voice
melting snow over branches, points
to the crunching doe across the ridge.[Z]

iii   As history is rather large and partial
the Norton Anthology compiles most
extra-contextual important fragments.
We were assigned *The Fairie Queen*
and *Oroonoko*; I can't recall a dot
of plot for I was the king's cupbearer.[S]

iv   A poisoned child, shores of Ohio,
poisoned the kiddies of Pontchartrain.
Poisoning children on banks of the Nile
to poison the child of the Mediterrain.
A poisoned child whose mother will cry, *oh!*
another aloft for His Kingdom to gain![Q]

v   The horse legs buckle under high
pressure air cartridge to the temple.
Two lamb rows drain blood from throat
slits, then lop heads and skin. Pigs
grumble into the gas showers. Barfing
teens champion veganism for a week.[M]

vi   Neither positive nor negative, rather,
mere color of paper, but connotation:
construct of black fear, spotless white.
The valley day passes, night same, and in
between. Each duration of sky ill-suits
compartments, surges in place in time.[L]

vii   How could a father withhold respect
from one child, favor the gifts of the other?
When the baby is born, the elder desires
to squash it in bathwater. This occurs
globally, though not to squirrels, snakes,
fish, or finches, the justified in fear.[J]

viii   We sped past Goleta that night
as CHP blocked the highway ahead.
The children feared the tunnel would
collapse. Trapdoor spiders. I drove
on calmly northbound into the earthquake, through fake stone, sanely home.

ix   The Towers intercept mothership signals:
remember bottles shattered in gutters,
overturned cruisers, temporarily inconvenienced
Korean convenience stores. Role model update.
Every ten minutes the train stops in Watts
where burrowed disquiet shatters, shatters.

x   Since the adolescence of an uncle died
the chest sat sealed by wooded bedside.
Inside might have been Han Solo,
Millenium Falcon, R2 and Greedo,
or Garfield plush with plastic eyes,
sealed by the mother in spring '85.[H]

xi   The distance from city limit to city
limit, six miles, from one edge
of the village to the wall of the next.
The childhood homestead view
of vultures in eucalyptus, viewed
by voyeurs in the shower afternoon.[D]

^Z grizzly bear/turtle hole/fire road/bridge

^S ruined home / Nehemiah / self-addressed / prayer⁺

^Q Mother Goose / apocrypha / diary / stain

^M carnival / slaughterhouse / ribosome / chic

^L discipline / marginal / metalworks / rhyme

^J Jupiter / paradise / son of a / tear

^H medical / Spanish Bay / calico / writhe

^D butternut / Monterey / octopus / strewn

⁺ The Fires
Recede, the Gates
Consumed with Water

Rotation

OLIVIA WU

land east and land west
with an ocean in between
east of land east is land west
west of land west is land east
both rotate around the same axis
from west towards east
if land west and land east
merge into one seamless entity
both lands will be irreconcilably disturbed
ocean preserves not only the boundary
but also the individuality of the duality

above the ocean, thunders ricochet after the lightening
teeming with whirling foams of spring
encapsulating generation after generation
the bewildering embedded in our gene
partially awakening, partially still spinning
veiled in inferiority never ending
but to what extent shall we be exposing
(I can't draw the line) such a suppression in hiding?
from west towards east, spinning, but not merging

at the center of the rotating sphere
neither fear nor fearless
neither love nor hatred

neither east nor west
neither forward nor backward
but it is not directionless
as both east and west move towards the sun and the moon
at the center, the axis is pure stillness without rotation
yet surrounded by pure rotation
east and west without distinction
spinning out longing & withholding wrapped in
silky threads of ambivalence & clarity
without paper or metal currency
spinning out nameless energy
and sleepless dreams escaping gravity

if you chase after west from the east
east's west is east, east remains east
west is never west from the perspective of east
west will always be west to those knowing the west
east and west rotate around the axis to spin out determination
there is no determination
yet through rotation there is only determination
east and west, through rotation, there is no distinction

As a Child, Drawing Purgatory

JOHN SIBLEY WILLIAMS

August: the road vagues, steams. This fractured center line seems to lead us into singed fields. Trucks roll fiery into ditches and are right to do so. Everything is right in doing what it does. Drunk on unencumbered sun the horizon stumbles between mountain peaks like an overpollinated bee, like how other people remember my grandfather.

*

Sky: an emptied womb. All the children here are grown or never were. All the birds, sung out. Sometimes I admire that nothing stays new for long. Boys pretend to be lots of things but yesterday was the first time I feigned motherhood. Each frog mucked up from the lake I cradled between my hands, taught to speak exactly how I speak, for a moment becoming larger than I am. Sky as an empty womb, I see it now. I see you by the dark and weedy pond out back, Mom, weeping over frog song, trying to keep the world in check.

*

August, and I am learning secondhand smoke from not-too-distant brushfires and cigars. Porchside, as I draw the world as I'd like it to be, from the outside looking in, my family talking around me like magpies, constant, staccato, deaf to what the world hears when it hears us. *If* is a question too abstract for such endless summer twilight. They say *when*, as in *when* the cancer takes her and *when* the fires eventually burn cold. When I grow up they say I'll resemble my grandfather, who always looked to me like a tattered scarecrow, like a cracked leather belt so worn it feels like skin against me.

*

We have been here before, at least in gesture. Stars thrown around the sky like toys I've left scattered across the living room for people bigger than me to trip over. Fruit bats complain from the vague upward darkness, and an oak tree that's seen wars begin and end around it sawed down to stump for winter fire. There is a bright white light inside I need to get out of my system. I need to break deeper than bone, take the stairs in twos and threes, swim farther from the pond's edge than I can safely return. And sometimes I need to kill something. Sometimes anything is better than waiting in waning heat for the cold to return with its smaller, controlled fires. In six months, when we thaw, the porch and smoke and uncertain highway will be like unopened buds, memories like tractors kicking up chaff and black birds. And I am tired of waiting. I am tired of waiting to be that scarecrow.

For Harry Dean Stanton

JOHN CLINTON

Harry Dean,

who *is* America
& its cheapest suit

hanging from the noose

of a lamented heartland.
haunting

the gas station sandwiches
& Old Milwaukee's

drunk
in front of
snowy televisions

pouring his guts out

to junkyard angels
on radioactive blacktops

with the vernacular of
canyon echos

tumbleweed mumbling
the rosary

with a weather
beaten face that bleeds

like the idealistic
union man of

some Rockwell
painting; in a landscape

of suicidal drifters,
you served society

& cinema as a character

actor piercing America
with the gospel of

your eyes.
may you never see

the day
this conglomerated country
has no need

for your wallflower
kind.

Cornering The Corner Market

ROGER APLON

Never can tell what'll rise to the bait when you toss out a hook & line & sure enough here's where the game gets good: one by one they come from the past to join in & divvy-up the spoils & out-of-the-box pops Jesse in her birthday suit & marches right up & demands attention which she gets from all the boys & some of the girls & *Strangers Welcome* is tattooed on her ass & *Tony & Bob* are the tats on her tits & 'the trouble that follows' leaves the scene before it starts & we march to the end of the hall to spy on Ruby who entertains fellow travelers & has been known to sell reefer on the side & sure enough when the door opens there's Big Bill himself strumming his Stratocaster, Artie T on bass & Joey-The-Mole on skins & at the center Bertha's passing shots of J T S Brown for old times sake & before we even blink it's our time for a good humor & a kiss on the cheek & toy poodles & all we can carry down to the car & off we go to the market where 'the rest is history' staggers past the yogurt & 'don't count your chickens' plays virtual pinball & 'fools rush in' sprints past the roasting chickens & it's not like it was & may never be again & we all chime in to say Hallelujah—just like that—in our best baritone . . . Hallelujah!

Green Eggs I Am

CHRISTIAN GEORGESCU

I did not spit in your green eyes and ham
it up so how come spam I am

I did not sit
I did not stop
I did not quit
I did not start
To even think of stopping
So how come half I am
A quarter an eighth an ounce
Of my former self
A name I can no longer even pronounce

I do not like it
I do not like it
I do not like this life
Not in the morning b4 the 9 to 5
Not in the evening at the   5 to 9
I do not like it
I do no like it
I do not like this life one bit

I do not like it
I do not like it
I do not like my face one bit
Not for a minute not a sec
Just makes me sic sic sic

Green Eggs and Ham ming it up
For your affection I am

I do not like
I do not like
I do not like
How dependent I am
On your approval and attention
How despondent I am
When you are so resplendent
Am I not splendid too

Or is that repulsive
Or is that responsive

Or is that depraved
Dear God d ess
Why won't you respond
I am wont to calling out your name
        wont to searching out your face

I am not at home
I am not at home
I am not at home
In this house
Not even w a double click of a mouse
I am not home in this house

When I look in the mirror
All I see is green eggs and ham
How unSame I am
How inSane I am
I do not like how I am
Less than green eggs and ham
Less than a gram of bacon
Here lies the faking

Gulp Gulp go the meds
Like a pez dispenser
Back goes the head
Gulp Gulp go the meds

I know I can
I know I can
I know I can
Do better than this

I know I am
I know I am
I know I am
So much better than this
Green w envy
Begging
for the I AM

Narcissists Anonymous

ANTON YAKOVLEV

My name is Paul Grand III, and I'm a narcissist.
I live on a boat, and I write screenplays.
I'm self-important about those things.
I cross the Hudson each morning, you know how much effort that takes?
Anyone that doesn't live on a boat has it easy.
I write screenplays to come to terms with that fact.

Because I write screenplays, I cut in line at the grocery store.
The quarrels and the ass-kicking that follow
fuel my righteous indignation
and give me plenty of colorful characters to write about.
My favorite was the grandmother with a head of lettuce
who tried to kick me but kicked the bucket instead.

I don't have a land line, what with living on a boat.
Because of that, my cell phone time is twice as valuable.
I do want friends, so I give out my number to everybody,
but when they call me, my narcissism kicks in
and I never feel that taking the call is worth my time.
I write screenplays about that too, the tragic ones.

The same happens when someone asks me out on a date.
I'd love to accept—but damn it, I'm too important!
I never even say a word, I just walk away.
I've probably burned some bridges with that behavior.
I try not to think about that stuff.
A man like me should need no bridges.

It's very hard for me to walk up the stairs:
if there is anyone else on the stairs, I have to grab them
and throw them down, they do not deserve
to get to the top before I do, or even after I do.
I can spend hours on a single stair,
throwing people down and never reaching the top myself.

I hate being a narcissist. I suffer so much from it.
I'd like to learn humility in my bones, but I worry
no one will help me. Take yourselves, for instance—
look at you people, with your stubble and cubic zirconia!
You think your camaraderie will save me?
Think *you* are narcissists? Don't make me puke!

I don't even know why I bother talking to you.
I despise you. You're a total waste of my time.
Hold your condescending understanding.
I'm done here. You have questions? I will not answer.
I'll see you in hell. And don't you *dare* break into applause.
Nobody knows the narcissism I've been through.

Easter and I Take What You Have Given Me

NATASHA KOCHICHERIL MONI

Hunky Jesus Contest, Dolores Park, San Francisco, 2009

Everywhere men wore their crosses
as lawn ornaments.

        I collapsed.

Above me, the legs of strangers
and you let me fall

completely. My head against
a lawn of Hallelujahs.

      Somewhere
on a nearby hill

a bunny
clutches a basket

of chocolates. Here, I learn
to distrust anyone who bears

      breasts before supper.

Rock 'n' Roll Heart Attack

PUMA PERL

I was having a bad day. There'd been no heat or hot water for two weeks, a cold snap had hit the city, and I'd grown weary of dragging my towels and clean clothes from one friend's house to another. Feeling like I had not one social bone left in my body, I'd heated four pots of water and taken a lukewarm bath in a tub barely one quarter full. At least I didn't have to talk to anyone. Or so I thought.

Feeling disgruntled and not quite clean, I dressed in layers and headed to civilization, which was anywhere but home, when the cell phone rang.

It was aging rocker guy, the one with the blue-black hair and a marked disinterest in anything not rock and roll. Which, on some days, were most things.

My left arm's numb and tingling, he announced without preamble.

Are you at the hospital? I asked.

No...

Then you're waiting for an ambulance?

No...

You're telling me that despite the fact that you've already had two heart attacks, when your left arm numbs and tingles you call ME instead of 911? Is that what you're telling me?

Well, I thought it might go away.

When did it start?

During the night! I haven't slept! I've been worried about it!

During the night! And you're sitting there worrying and calling me? What can I do? Even if we weren't 3,000 miles apart, do you think I could fix this?

Okay, you're right . . . I'll walk over to the hospital.

You'll WALK over to the hospital? The hospital's five miles away!

No, it's 3.7 miles, I checked.

For the purpose of clarity, I shall inject the fact that aging rocker guy has lived in Los Angeles for twenty-seven years and has never learned to drive. His pool of friends willing to chauffeur him around has dwindled due to both natural attrition and his demands that they avoid freeways, drive no faster than thirty miles per hour, and keep the radio muted at all times. Since bus and taxi drivers are also generally unwilling to follow his orders, he has no choice but to walk everywhere.

Whatever! Call 911! You already owe them two and a half million dollars from your other heart attacks, what's another thousand for an ambulance?

It's one thousand, eight hundred.

What's the difference? Listen, call me from an emergency room or don't call me at all!

Boy, you're mean. And we're not even married, yet.

We're not getting married! I told him for the hundredth time. *Now go handle your business.*

I slammed the cell phone shut as hard as I could without damaging it, and momentarily longed for the days of sturdy black table models—when you hung up on someone with one of those babies, they knew you meant business.

Several hours later, he called again, sounding chipper.

I'm feeling better, he informed me.

What did the doctors say? I asked.

I didn't go.

You didn't go????

No, I called Johnny Pompadour for a ride, and he said maybe I just pulled something and to rub some BenGay on it and now it feels better.

Oh—you called DOCTOR Johnny Pompadour, the heavy metal moron who lives further in the past than you do, and listened to his advice?

Well . . . it's not tingling as much . . .

AS MUCH? Maybe DOCTOR Pompadour could pay a house call and assess the tingling sensation and make further recommendations? Or maybe you could just go to the fucking hospital?

Why are you getting so upset?

You've had two heart attacks in the past, you're ignoring the signs of another one, and you're consulting stupid, eyeliner-wearing Johnny Pompadour instead of just going to Cedar Mt. Sinai, which saved your sorry ass twice—THAT's why I'm getting upset!

Well, I was scared . . . I already told you, I was up all night worrying about it.

That's a reason? I raised two kids—I don't need to adopt a senior citizen rocker who stays home for twenty-four hours worrying instead of taking care of himself, and who relies on his heavy metal buddy Johnny Pompadour as his medical consultant!

I hate heavy metal! You know how much I hate heavy metal.

WHATEVER!

I can't believe I just yelled "Whatever" at somebody. Over the last two months, my Aunt Alma died, I lost my job and my health insurance, my Aunt Ruth died, my son broke his ankle, and my daughter lost her apartment and everything in it to an electrical fire. I had run out of relatives and kids. No way was I becoming caretaker to a black Levi skinny jean wearing sixty-five-year-old who didn't even have it together to get Medicare, even if he does hate heavy metal and loves the Beatles.

Okay, you're right, he finally agreed. *I'm going to the hospital.*

That's what you said twelve hours ago! Do what you want; don't even tell me about it.

Boy, you're mean. Now I know you love me. Otherwise, you wouldn't be so upset.

I didn't bother to answer. Several hours later, he called again, happily watching television in his hospital bed. Apparently, there had been something to Johnny Pompadour's analysis. After running a battery of tests, they had concluded that during his Hogan's Heroes marathon at his computer (his television was broken) he had kept his left arm tucked away in some weird position, not moving for hours. His doctor's orders were to tear himself away from his YouTubes and sit-coms and walk around every half hour or so. He was a little bit sad about being released—although the hospital hadn't provided the flat screen he longed for, it was better than what he had in his apartment.

I'll call you when I get home, he said.

Can't wait, I thought.

True to his word, he called, regaling me with the details of his conversations with doctors and nurses, during which he'd managed to reference conversations with Shelia E and Robin Zander and drop Neil Young's name twice.

Did you eat? I asked out of habit. I seem to always be asking people if they ate, even on days when I live on peanut butter and apples.

I'm going to make some broccoli and brown rice.

That's what he eats every day.

You could vary your vegetables, you know, I told him. I always said that. I don't why I can't stop myself from saying things like that.

You're such a nag. And we're not even married yet.

We're not getting married! I yelled for the hundred and first time, and opened a new jar of peanut butter.

LOVE 1A:

JARED SINGER

Love can only be described
the way it is lived. In parts.

Hoping that the whole makes sense,
even though we know none of the pieces do.

Love 1A:
Love *is* a sandwich. Both are surprisingly
delicate things easily ruined by reckless hands.
We put both in our mouths.

Love 1B:
I fuck like a hurricane,
this is to say nothing of its volume or its sudden onset,
only that it requires an entire team of scientists to
predict when it will happen.

I love like a tornado,
in here we will be safe.

But around us, things will be destroyed
by our excess, and I promise, we will not end
up in the same place that we started.

Love 1C:
If there is anything more like the way I fall in love
then a children's cartoon, I haven't found it yet.

There are eight women who say that I am the perfect man,
that any woman would be lucky to have me.
I have asked three of them out.
They all said no, we still hang out

but boy it gets awkward sometimes.
If there is anything more like a painting
of a tunnel on a wall than this,
I haven't found it yet.

Love 2:
Love is the only thing that all of the songs are right about.

Love 3:
The heart is a terrible metaphor
for love, please stop using it.
Love is not a muscle,
it cannot atrophy from lack of use.
Love is an organ, it can always sneak up on you.

The lungs are a much better metaphor for love.

The inhale is that moment of excitement when you know the
joke is funny but you aren't laughing because there never
seems to be enough air to laugh, or speak, when they look at you.

The exhale that moment when it fails, when your eyes meet
and you have to pretend you don't know each other.

But the holding, that moment
when your body is all potential. That is love.
Love is

The Bust

RON KOLM

Years ago I got fired from a shitty low-paying job at the Strand Bookstore—but it was for a crime I didn't commit. I was working the cash register in the front of the store, and noticed an expensive leather-bound set of Dickens' letters, wrapped in brown paper, on the counter in front of me. I figured it had been sent down from the Rare Books Room on the fifth floor and was waiting for a customer to come in and pick it up. It was an extremely slow day, so I started doodling with a ballpoint pen on the wrapping.

From out of nowhere, two hands appeared, grabbed at the parcel and tried to snatch it from the counter. I held it in place and looked up to see what was going on. I was surprised to find myself staring at the face of an ex-employee. This particular ex-employee was a strange dude from the mid-west who wore size 17 shoes, and resembled Civil War soldiers I'd seen in old photographs. I sometimes thought that if reincarnation was real, that's what he had been.

And he was a thief—a very clever thief. He was in charge of taking books that had been ordered by mail to the post office on Fourth Avenue, and paying to have them shipped to out-of-state customers. On one of his trips he'd reached into a postal clerk's window when his back was turned, and scooped up a receipt book. He would pay, let's say, fifty dollars for a mailing, write seventy-five on his own copy of the receipt, tossing away the real one, and pocket the difference. He'd then take his mail cart over to the Albert Hotel on University Place where he lived, park it outside, take several bags of books he'd coveted (but hadn't paid for) up to his room, and then return to the store. He was efficient, so only a few of us knew what he was up to and, as we weren't snitches, nobody told on him. More to the point, he was very strong and very crazy, and those are the real reasons nobody spilled the beans. He was finally let go because one of the managers sort of suspected something, or just because he was so weird.

Anyway, he glared at me and told me he was taking the letters.

"Man, you can't do that! That's stealing! I'll get fired!"

"Oh, alright! Here you go," he said, tossing a crumpled-up ten dollar bill over the counter, where it fell to the floor. When I bent over to pick it up, he grabbed the package and left.

It turned out that the manager who had gotten him fired had been tailing him, witnessed the entire transaction, and thought I was in cahoots with the thief. So I got fired; no matter how much I protested and tried to explain what had really happened.

I filed for unemployment, but was told that my former employer was blocking any payments. I panicked. I was living pretty close to the edge, and the store wasn't paying me all that much as it was—I sure hadn't managed to save anything. I figured I might be able set things straight by getting the books back to the store. I had to do something, or I'd soon be living on the street. I took a couple of friends along, in case things got physical, and went over to the Albert Hotel. My friends kept out of sight in the stairwell while I banged on his door.

Much to my surprise, he opened the door and let me in. His room was unfurnished—there was just this massive pile of books and boxes in the center of the floor, which was bare. There seemed to be some kind of sleeping bag next to it with a blanket strewn on top. I looked around, still kind of surprised to be there, and noticed that there was a mantel on the wall to the right of the door over a fake fireplace, with stuff on it—some candles and what looked like a bust. I walked over for a closer look and discovered that it was a black marble bust of Adolf Hitler. I mumbled something or another about my financial situation, and how desperate I was, but I couldn't focus; I was shaking. He seemed to sense my extreme unease, and must have felt sorry for me, because he gave me back the Dickens, still wrapped in the brown paper covered with my doodles.

I clutched the package and staggered out into the hallway feeling like I'd been punched in the chest by a massive fist.

Body Tattoo

GEORGE GUIDA

> *"The official Twitter account for the Palm Beach County Alerts . . . tweeted that the naked gunman was on the roof acting 'psychotic' while 'rolling around the floor' threatening to shoot whoever comes within eyesight."*

What energy hummed from the blue skin of biceps-twining serpents
scarified with family names, fangs above wrist, wrestled with
in thinking how he covered every inch of flesh over time, flesh
darkened to target shades of other arms, and gunstocks in their mouths.

He would lift it to a sky above the roof. The spotlights would show
the barrel. The vessel of scripture would glow with Vishnu.
His spark would return to the Universe, survive in spears of grass
and stray cats prowling without judgment. For each of them, a rose

on the chest; on the back, meteors soon dust, his force released,
his spirit painted cats' eyes. Lucky to die this way, the prophets said.
The painted signs, the roof, the first footfall, the pop and sting
like a hundred artists' needles snapped off in the flesh.

Breathless

ALEJANDRO ESCUDÉ

You're going there now—that night in cold Buenos Aires
with your father as the rest stayed behind in the restaurant, you'd taken

final strides toward marriage and Father took a drag of his cigarette
and smiled at you and the Argentinians didn't know what to say

to these two Americans—ha!, so immigration is a punk rock song
played in the grayness of a relinquished city, Father a lovely man

with a bald head and a mighty temper to leave them breathless.
Oh liberation! The nice old couple who wished you both

buenos noches, he and you listening to the oracular sirens wail
on the other side of 9th of July Boulevard, you could hear

the fading death-pulse of the military junta, you could feel it
succumb to the duo of enduring immigrants having returned home

to Buenos Aires just for a few weeks, skyscrapers like boxes
full of corpses, his cigarette smoke taken by a sudden lash of wind.

Rain

SOODABEH SAEIDNIA

There is rain pouring
Rain is pouring with rage
Rain is pouring inside your skull
Rain is pouring on Michael Kors in the woman's fist

The rain and the Michael Kors are both pouring
on my bare bones
Rain is shamelessly pouring
Rain can send you home
with the woman and her Micheal Kors
Rain is furiously watching my fears
I bury myself under your arms
But rain tickles my nose

Rain turns red
Rain is bloody
dripping on your hands and turning off your Marlboro
wiping your face, kissing your lips
It's just an ordinary rain in NYC, you say
flirting with the rain's eyes
But at the same time, rain turns purple
wrinkles your forehead

Rain was already my friend
but now, approaches my neck and presses tightly
I'm feeling suffocated

Angry rain and its pressure are going up
throwing up
Madness is pouring
Madness is pouring with rain

You shock and become silent
Rain and Madness turn black
Rain and Madness are putting on your pants
getting out of your nostrils
Black rain who gets out of your nose
Madness who gets out of the woman's dress
Black rain and Madness fill the subway
Black rain and Madness kill a boy by mistake
A boy who looks like my prince

Rain turns green
Rain reads the commercials on the wall and laughs
The rain and the woman are looking at your nose
There is blood coming out
Blood is pouring, but at the same time
turns white and translucent
I breathe out safely

It is raining
Rain is dripping on my shoes
My shoes are Payless
I respectfully invite the rain into my shoes' party
My toes embrace the rain warmly
and blush
You walk with the woman shoulder to shoulder
Rain is still caressing my cheeks
The rain and I are dripping

Drawing Blanks

VIVIAN FAITH PRESCOTT

White Indigenous people are _____ .

All Sámi love reindeer because _____ .

You aren't Indigenous because you don't live _____ .

If you don't know how to yoik you are _____ .

Drawing blanks is like shooting blanks is like being draped in fur blankets at night. Unlimited coverlet encased and overspreading the empty space. you face your face. Blankety-Blankety-blank. That blank look that wrapped you and shot through you. You make a blanket statement.

If you think Santa Claus is the most widespread misappropriation
of culture in history you are _____ .

You are Indigenous because _____ .

Your ancestors lived in teepees because _____ .

You have the urge to migrate because _____ .

Your tongue is blank. You are quite. quiet. when the molecules in the room refer to whiteness. Every day you sense your ladder twisting to a spiral. Nothing is certain except when it is. As a kid you blanked out. Teachers yelled at you for it. You still stare ahead and are frequently asked what is the matter or what the matter is.

You are quiet when watching the northern lights because _____

_____ .

You can't speak your indigenous tongue because _____ .

Shamanism is _____ .

You are fascinated with the sun and wind because _____ .

But matter is the matter and it is nothingness that you go to. Migrate toward. But you know that matter is the histories we are made of. Void. gap. break. empty space. erase. erase. erase. This trancelike state. Blank.

Fill it in. Instill it. Uninstall it. This uncomfortable skin you're in. Has been colonized for hundreds of years. Fall through it. You are still. On this migration. We say it is *baiki*, the home we carry with us. Nomadic peoples. No madness. This migration.

Your traditional clothing consists of _____ .

Your National Geographic DNA sequence proves _____ .

Part of your history is blank because _____ .

You are using that blank stare because _your ancestors could fall into trances_ .

This Poem Has No Mother

DEBORAH HAUSER

my mother / my meadow / if I could mint money / my nemesis / would be properly
medicated / and wouldn't cry over spilt milk / or manacle herself to a man in exchange
for a mink stole and a hallmark greeting card / make no mistake / she managed to serve
meals / the meat tenderly seasoned / movie moms are less maudlin than mine / muddy
waters ran over that formica countertop with the metal edge trim / mad, mean, morose /
mauve carpets failed to comfort / the house was a tomb / maternity a massive error /
the moving men are here / leave no marks.

Checking through the Blinds

ANNIE SAUTER

Every sensible woman got a back-door man.
—Sara Martin

Checking the blinds
I smile, alright a little
Jealously, but really, sort of
More just smiling, *for*
You and your *get-*
Over-ways, your rural decay
Teeth always forming,
Your own

Perfect smile.

How's trix, we say
In passing, *hey*
Pretty lady, beneath
Your frosted breath,
I kick shut the hatchback
And climb in the car
        I am going to the gym and
        Will have zero flab left, by
The time I return
To him, and NYC

When the snow melts.

Her car, parked
Outside her place. Her husband
Still—not here. Yet.

I guess I got too used
To being so far away
So far from mind or
Sight that I forgot
Here, we might get caught. Being

Caught, sounding so
Foreign, as if we were
French lovers meeting
On the famous river's edge

In an endless fog,
—Not merely two old-people,
—Drunk and tired
Eating soft-boiled eggs
On a neck-breaking
Couch at noon.

Caught? What? Like fish
On a stringer, or
in a bucket, doomed
And resigned? Caught?

Doing what? Having bloody
Desperate sex as if our lives
Depended

On getting off?

I can't comprehend it, so
I guess my smile for you

Is genuine. I really am
Glad for you—and that you
Are over there
With her—Better her
Than me,

When the newspaper headlines
Read *"Shooting at*
Trailer Park."

Or *"Younger man shoots*
Geriatric husband
Of Missouri woman—
Caught in torrid love
Triangle."

Well of course you do.

But, I am going back to NYC in
The spring. Yeah, dressed in black,
But not in mourning—dressed in
No flab, not even any
Left, on my arms or stomach.

No bullet holes either.

Been there
Done that. Decades ago.
        —Being all shot at in a
        Trailer—

So, now, I can smile.
For you, and know

You really are one lucky
Back-door man.

You're a Fairy Boy Slag

PRUDENCE CHAMBERLAIN

More masculine girls have more lovers whether they are straight or gay.
—Daily Mail

The old silence
of an unlit bus;
this city
is ancient   I know
I look at you like this puppied
thing & I like you
by chance
            a brute that owns me
because I love your size & toughness
 when I am young canine & spiked

We as a
bell & a ball
eye one
another
rapturously
rolling sounds
around the
train station's
Victorian heights

And there is no hope
            between our bodies
I know who I am

writing love to
when I am alone

so that when I am cash-in-hand
you ask me
          do you want to be a team of cleaners?
Do you want to be a star?
We can have arbitrary Tuesdays with coffee
mornings
          as my whole week turns on loneliness;
an office job for everyone

There is so much
          too much
to collapse me into your
wingspan & feed me stolen
shine
          what I feel with
you is pure animal &
take you as a face value love

when you talk about my tomboy
gene   your whole hand   holds
across the exaggerated lock of my ankle
& sometimes
I forget our sized
differences   that you could pocket me
but don't   & instead

listen before you tell me

if I will not self-define as feminine
I can pass as a fairy-boy   where I want
no lover other than you.

The Rain Broke
My Kale

DAWN Z. MONTEFUSCO

snapped it like
a toothpick,
a child's dream,
a friend dying,
all at once, no kale.

I tried to protect it,
the same way I
guard my pride.
I was married once.
The divorce burned a hole
in my cerebral cortex
like a lobotomy.

I'm just like the kale now,
Shattered.
So many directions.

The lettuce is still okay though,
its leaves inconsequential and dumb.
I like lettuce.

Tomorrow I will plant arugula,
and hope the bitter leaves
don't break.

Encounter

JILL S. RAPAPORT

And so passed many uneventful days, after Miss Maynish went her way and the house was aired out. A summer came, and fall, the winter with its holidays, and then the spring again, through a long, slow tunnel of chill nights and days finally nearing an opening into sunlight and budding leaves. Peggi crossed the big street this time from south to north, the opposite of the way she had when Miss Maynish was still out in Thistle Island; away from rather than toward the second-story statue of a Roman Joan of Arc lifting her staff contemplatively as she extended one graceful leg in front of her and deliberated on military matters. The fruit seller reappeared toward the end of April, having spent all the cold months absent. Looking west down the long thoroughfare, one saw again the lacey bridges and some fishnet tenting, trucks softly rumbling amid dapplings of late-day sun.

"Miss Peggi! How are you?" a woman cried, approaching as the light was about to change; Peggi looked up and noticed that it was either stop and miss it or race to make it and ignore the friendly greeting. She focused her eyes on the lady and tried to think where she'd seen her before, because she had. Tillie Slocum, who had come on weekends from July to September, then quit to go back to her own country because the company hadn't been paying enough. "Hi," said Peggi with a sudden feeling of affection. "How's Miss M.?" Tillie asked.

The question was experienced as a physical blow. Miss M. had gone off in late May, Memorial Day weekend. But such information need not be handed out randomly. Peggi had earlier that week cut short a long interrogation from an Eric S. of United Bancard trying to help her process a credit card application for which, inexplicably, he seemed to think he needed her mother's maiden name as a security password at the very end, when he had already amassed enough information on her to track her every transaction in the world till the end of the world, and she had bailed out at that last request, feeling that the mother's maiden name as a security password was not something Eric should properly have been asking for in addition to all the rest; in the old days, the security password came at the so-called back end of the credit application, once the card had been granted and mailed and received. To ask for it before sending the card seemed to defeat the whole purpose of security in credit.

So now, when Tillie Slocum wanted to find out how Miss Maynish was, and might have been digging around for more (although Peggi knew underneath it all somehow that she wasn't), Peggi considered what she might do to avoid answering.

Then a car squealed and someone else cried her name out and suddenly she said to Tillie, "She died at the end of May."

Albert Nord came up and put his hand on her shoulder just at that moment; it was he who had called to her. And she looked at Tillie, who seemed disconcerted, whose brown eyes had filmed over, and who seemed unsure what to do next, and then turned to Albert and said hello.

He looked at the stricken Tillie and entered into the frieze, and the light, most animated of any of them, allowed its liveliness to ebb moment by moment and perceptibly, so that a moment of redirection of the gaze from this storefront to that side of a truck to, if luck provided, the striped body of the proprietor's cat in front of the corner market meant that when the gaze returned to the original surface upon which it had lingered, the sun, having painted that place in rich tones just before, had altogether left a moment or less than a moment later, after the wandering eyes had made their tour and come home again.

The fruit seller, Peggi noted, was not the same young Turkish guy of the previous spring, summer and early fall; now it was a more hardened-looking type, maybe the guy who had been there before the Turkish guy. The truck, right under Joan of Arc, had been there throughout the seasons for years, but only this past year disappeared when the weather got colder. It was a year in which a lot of things had changed and disappeared.

Albert shivered and looked appealingly at her. Tillie gathered her forces. Peggi felt the whirl of white dust chips, and tangles of hair and fur and leaves, twigs, bits of bracken, bits of fallen strawberry and blueberry, scraps of rubber tire from blowouts and accidents, slivers of painted metal, blow around her in a turbid hoop.

Tillie, who had seemed pretty months ago, now reminded her of Hilda, who just two nights ago had chattered on without stopping or letting anybody else get a word in edgewise and peppered everybody who dared to speak with BB-gun blasts of stupid and irrelevant questions designed to render them speechless so that she could resume holding the floor on the rare occasions when she had inadvertently lost it for a brief spell. Finally Peggi had stopped her by saying, "Could I just interrupt you for a moment to ask you why you're doing what you just accused this lady (sorry, I've forgotten your name) of doing: talking a blue streak and killing us all with details?" The lady whose name she'd forgotten sort of raised her hand and said, "Dee," and Hilda simply stared, having for once been met by a sentence to which she did not have an instant and electrifying riposte. In fact she was rarely, no, *never* really anything other than constantly chattering and endlessly insistent. But Hilda was Hilda and Tillie was Tillie, a gentler woman entirely. And let's not forget Dee, who had her own way of sending up whirls of smoke and dust.

Tillie and Peggi now inwardly saw a paper image of Miss M., and watched again as she made her way into the distance, amid soft air and the scent of green and pink.

6 Short Films

MAW SHEIN WIN

1
A long shot of a woman's shins wrapped in cotton gauze.
Red maple tree outside the window and below the balcony.
A bowl of lemons on the neighbor's porch.

2
A blindfold wound around a man's bleeding head.
Wide angle view of a playground, children playing kickball in the dirt.
Hummingbirds captured in soft light.

3
The ending starts at the beginning.
Sound of a couple arguing in a restaurant.
Or the other way around.

4
Her pupils of soft brazen green.
Many bees escaped from the colony.
A murder mystery for a limited audience.

5
The soft tissue under his armpits.
Laughter in the bedroom.
An abandoned farm and a deserted mall.

6
Hand-held camera scenes of a college reunion.
A chronicle of one woman's journey through Tibet.
The factory workers assembling toy soldiers and ballerinas.

Surrogate

KATIE HIBNER

We found the babylift plastered on her honey nut forehead.
She was at the arts n crafts table, fashioning mint keychains and sodium armbands.

It was like she was only window-shopping,
zoning out while discussing sphincter politics
and cutting corner pieces for the tots.

We wanted to inject a bronco into her Jacuzzi,
but we needed to keep the war drowned at the day spa,

so we remained extracts,
dripping into her stadium
like pearls.

Treble in Mind

With a sense of urgency

Joel Allegretti

The letters of the following poem correspond sequentially
to the notes of the musical composition.

Ecce a cab! A fab cab.
Face a cab—beg a cab.
Cab fad!
Dead cab?
A bad cab! A cad cab!
Ecce! *Ecce*!
Bag a cab, Gabe.
Da-da! Da-da!
Da-dee!!!

Assemblages III

BRENDA YATES

Conditional References

Bipolar enthusiasms are extremely sad

Semantic properties are dependent on circumstance

Conclusions aren't any more of an end than intersections of woof and warp on a loom

Another way of putting this is different

If then were otherwise, similar would look more familiar

A tension between is more like taffy than glue

Simple or complex representations, at first just aspects, may, or even often, become doctrine

Modes of derivation are inferior to patterns of migration, don't you agree?

Finally, for better or worse, putting intractable words down

contextualizes

The Deer

MIKE MORAN

I

I want to be the deer now
and go leaping over from dusty ditch
to unharvested corn.
It's a rough-n-tumble need to tear my flesh on the barbed wire of farmyard fences,
and a tailflick desire to feed and feed and feed in tall grasses.
Yeah, I know the hunters are out there on the other side of the ditches, rolling over the
　　　gravel roads in their american-built pick-up truck and waiting for me.

But everybody's got pressures, right?

II

I want to be the hunter sitting in the passenger seat next to my buddy now, don't I?
Yeah, and it's his truck, but I'm holding the rifle and I know the deer is in there,
　　　somewhere in that field.
"Mebbe we should let it feed and fatten up a bit," my buddy suggests.
Shut up, I want to say, but I don't say jack.

I want that deer.

I can see it now.
It's a doe and I can only see one.

My buddy doesn't see it.

My buddy's a blind idiot.

III

I want to be the truck now, forget the hunter.
Crunching up the grit and the gravel under my tires and mud on my flaps and all four
        wheels spinning—that's me.
I'm ready to jump this goddammed ditch and just go tearing through the fence and
        straight into the field.
What the hell do I care for corn?

I want to be able to go where the pussycars on the highways can't go.
I want to tear across the cornfield and leave a wrecked and broken path behind me.
I want to spit dark soil out from all four tires, engaged and furious.
I want to run that deer down
while the two men bouncing around in my cab like a couple of angry thoughts whoop and
        scream and explode their bullets from their rifles.

IV

I want to be the cornfield sometimes though, too—
still
and straight
and full.

I want to be shadowed, rustling lanes
of tumbled black dirt
and whispery golden leaves.

I want to shelter the animal—
the rabbit and the spider and the raccoon.
I want to give home to the snake and the gopher.

I want to grow fat ears under a hot sun,
blistering, lush ears of straight cob and yellow-white kernels
all wrapped up tight like a secret in cornsilk
and green leaf.

I want to offer the random bites of food
to the deer now moving
quiet through my rows.
I want to stroke her sides with tickling caresses,
even as the truck
comes cutting through my edgerows, barreling down on her.

V

I want to be the bullet.
I want to be the thing thrust into the narrow black chamber.
I want the singleness of purpose given me as the hammer blasts against my ass and
        explodes me into a spin through the long shaft and then out,
shooting, blasting, screaming, flying into sunshine and over earth;
splitting and shattering corn leaves
and then striking

with power and purpose
into the side of the deer.
I want to feel the crust of fur and flesh as I slam out of sunlight
and thrust my way into red darkness,
slicing through the strands of muscle,
catching a bit of bone, a bit of rib,

and feeling it break even as it redirects my coursing spin deeper
into the bloody red power of life;
going straight again as I slow,
slow,
straight now
into the heart of the animal.

And I rest there and feel,
in my final thrusting, turning motion,
the grasp of heart muscle as it constricts,
tightens,
hugs,
and then holds me, finally,
still.

VI

And then will I be the dust:
thrown from stopped tires,
stirred from booted feet,
thumped up from fallen body.

Then will I billow up
across face and eyelash
and muddy the tears blinked out against me.

And then will I spread and settle—
like a gentle blanket, like gentle earth—
dusting the barbed wire of farmyard fences,
and laying down across the trail,
only just made with body and hoof,
that cuts through the tall grass
of the bordering ditch.

I Played God on a Thursday

JOHN W. SNYDER

It's a strange day
when your job demands a mercy killing.

Nobody thinks of the small things,
like suffocation,
like a night sky made of plastic.
I hope, dear fish,
that the last thing you saw
was the eyes of your dead brethren
twinkling like stars.

For you,
heaven is cold.
Most freezers
are not graveyards.

You have the luxury, dear fish,
of not having to pretend.
You don't have to take
two blue pills a day
and swim like everybody else.

You have the luxury, dear fish,
of being small.

You couldn't hold this burden
even if you tried.

You have the luxury, dear fish,
of no more luxuries.
They only get in the way of dying.

Pepper

for Mom (1980)

CHRIS WIEWIORA

Less than six months ago you had walked down the aisle of your home church, First United Methodist in Buckhannon, West Virginia, with your Chicagoan husband Rich Wiewiora. While he was used to diversified metropolises, LA wasn't your small country town, LA was the inner city. It felt divided. You could feel the lingering static from the previous year's riots. But it wasn't like you hadn't grown up with black folks—your freshman roommate was black—it was just that everyone was black there. And you, you were a white speck of salt.

LA was supposed to feel as different as you would be when you were overseas. Everyone spoke English, though. You were still in America no matter how radical and otherworldly it felt. And you really felt overwhelmed in your *How to Learn a Language* class that you and Rich took in the mornings at the host church. You were glad Rich knew Polish, had grown up with it, and maybe even still dreamed in it. Even though he had no accent, you knew he knew how to speak it. That was a comfort in that uncomfortable place.

Liz and Archie, the couple you were staying with, were required to provide you and Rich a bedroom and bathroom as well as breakfast and dinner. At lunch break between classes, you savored your PB&J because it was nothing like the peppered pork chops, peppered beans, peppered potatoes, peppered everything that Liz made. You couldn't stand it and your stomach couldn't handle it. After class, you would beg Rich to go to McDonald's so you could have a non-peppered quarter-pounder with cheese.

Your PB&J sustained you as you went on your afternoon rounds of the neighborhood. At each house's door, you knocked and then said, "We're from Faithful Central Missionary Baptist Church over on Hoover with Reverend Dr. Robinson. And we're seeing if you'd like to hear something about Jesus." You recited the script you had memorized to alleviate any worries about why you were there.

More often than not the folks who opened their doors knew the church or mentioned another one they said they attended. If they said that, then you asked, "Have you made the wonderful discovery of knowing Christ?" When they said that they hadn't committed to Christ, then you opened up the *Four Spiritual Laws* pamphlet and read through the steps with them.

Then you walked back to the sidewalk. Rich always did such a great job following a script, but also just listening. You couldn't argue with him about the pepper in Liz and Archie's house, because they would have heard you through the walls but also because Rich wouldn't argue. He'd take you to McDonald's and then kiss you with his mustache brushing your lips.

One Sunday at Faithful Central, you had noticed Rich's mustache moving with different words from the song as he danced down the aisles with the rest of the choir. He was supposed to be moving forward and dancing and singing, which was much too much for him all at once. You smiled, probably the only one who noticed him counting the steps instead of singing.

On the sidewalk, you bowed and then prayed out loud, "Dear Lord we just had a wonderful conversation . . . " At the same time, you prayed in your head, thanking God that Rich would be with you in Poland and he would be able to tell you what people were saying. When you were there, you planned to attend a church that didn't require him to dance and sing. Also, you'd go to McDonald's whenever you wanted and you'd never have pepper in your home. Out there in LA, you said, "Amen," asking God to let it be so.

Such feats of esoterica could give a soul malaria

SB STOKES

It was simple: there was no more carpet on the grass, on the lawn, all alone. The phone a mere figment, like the moon, alone late at night. The back recoils and sends the rest of the body packing, headlong, stacking up like the infractions of a bad boy band run amok. There's a haunting voice asking for redemption and a drunken master with his head gone wrong. Shake out the lampshades, shake out the carpets. The parapets all shout out his name at sunset on this thirteenth day. Another one away from the womb-like clasp of a brother's loving hands. The night bird's wings are songs made of sad flappings. The wind brings warm porridge and a promise, slipped to us right before sleep, like a damp card under a stormy night door. Unfold the worn paper and begin to sing with the ink that runs within.

Bending Spoons with Prayer Waves

CRAIG KITE

Warm fountain,
      Faith sculpted you from an ambulatory mountain.
And even your dog is a tributary
Gathered from the snow of angels combusting
On anxiety-ridden bedspreads,
   That happy beast
            That peed
                    On your carpet.

Warm fountain,
Where's the dress with black sequins you remember fitting
(Big perm, shoulder pads   hairspray in your lungs)
When you collected his sparse attention in your basin?

Your jewelry box detained patient doves who sang slow motion.
I was allowed to play with them and hang them from my neck.
I was pretty   And your stomach was: fluttering mariposas.
You tried to wash your hands of all the figments.
           Your hands would always bleed.
   Next to godliness:
          Unclean.

Spinning plates   Bending spoons   with prayer waves   Levitating
        through the ceiling of your kitchen

brandishing your hand wave Hi   down at ants in baffling traffic:
the buzz after a good cry   in the sink.

When I came to your door, you said,   "Baby, I'm just praying."
But it sounded like   you were
                                                losing
                                                your mind.

Warm fountain,
     You plan your garden   at the side of your house
               and are a heroine
with your collection of   refrigerator magnets   and mason jars,
preserves of wishes that weren't even yours, pectin punches, gelatin stars.

Monsanto will be a handful of mutinies sewn out fallow and the
bumbling lords of comfortable things will nap-sack corn-chip sadness
and snack on diabetes bugs in their man-cave den implosions, waking
themselves up from regret and the volume of their snoring.

Then, warm fountain, I can see you break your basin, refuse
responsibility for holding others' wishes, returning every coin
flipped with a fuck you and becoming hot spring, divorcee, blonde
hottie at 53, with headlight eyes, electric slide . . . before your mother
forgets her name.

How to Lie about Recovery

SARAEVE FERMIN

Buy locks, but no keys. Hide them where you used to stash
the donuts. Learn to drink cup after cup of black coffee,
let the caffeine churn your gut into silence, when you begin
to vomit up excuses, stuff them in the back of the underwear
drawer, with all of the bras that do not fit. Put all the knives
in a vase, or a decorated coffee can, become a celebration of
every wound, every scar, every bite. Relearn sunshine,
how to gag, how to use a question without flinching,
how to swallow an apology like rotten milk. Swat the flies
away from their compliments—"you look so much better . . . now . . .
before . . . in black . . . when you smile . . . in those pants . . . "
Take the 320 bus across the GWB, gaze longingly at the hospital
you gave almost a decade of your life to, play songs on
the collarbones you developed only when they couldn't find
a vein good enough to feed you liquids through anymore.
When everyone goes to bed, in the thickest night, the only
time you feel small enough not to matter, make your move.
Cut off your least desirable limb. Deliver it to her,
gift-wrapped. Ask the mirror, *Now, isn't that enough already?*

Chopsticks

CHANEL BRENNER

A gardener trims
      the lawn
            with a weed cutter.

The smell of grass knifes
      through the space
            below the door.

The mother is in the future
      of a poem
            she has already written.

It is the eighth anniversary
      of her son's
            death.

She sits at a table
      and picks up the letters of his name
            with chopsticks.

She chews and swallows
      each one, savoring
            the severed flavors.

In the poem a Japanese man vanishes
        and becomes
                kana on the wall.

Her poem is stone steps
        that people keep
                tripping over.

A wine glass
        breaks.
                Someone yells *fire*.

The woman wraps herself
        in her son's favorite blanket
                and eats rice with a fork.

A toddler sits across from her
        and picks up pieces of chicken
                with chopsticks.

It is silent
        and the smell of grass
                has turned to smoke.

Infinite Worlds

MARY MACKEY

The limitless content of our universe might be only one instance of a large (and possibly infinite) number of other universes.
> —Astronomer Seth Shostak, Director of the Center for SETI Research

When you lift your fork an infinite number of yous
all lift their forks at the same instant   and an infinite number
are missing their mouths   and an infinite number are choking
on the tines   and an infinite number are being struck by meteors
and vaporized   and an infinite number are being trampled by
cattle or time-traveling mammoths or naked strippers
who look like Martha Washington   and an infinite number
of the strippers are sprouting purple wings just as Christ
is coming back in the form of an infinite number of small green aliens
who are explaining they are a poetry collective that specializes in holographs
and apologizing for the cultural disruption their guy-on-the-cross
experiment made   and that fork keeps rising and rising and destroying
everything in its path as you commit suicide an infinite number
of times   and give birth to an infinite number of babies who drown
in an infinite number of great rivers 150 miles wide which suddenly
appear out of nowhere carrying schools of voracious piranhas who devour an
infinite number of yous forks before they turn into infinite numbers of gold, rats
hairpins and hockey sticks

because

when there are an infinite number of worlds anything can
happen   and will an infinite number of times   which is why
the idea of infinity   like all things that have no limits
is impossible to grasp even in your own kitchen over a plate
of fried potatoes with a red-handled stainless steel
fork

BOOTISM

RICHARD LORANGER

After what feels like months in my room,
talking to the bookshelves,
gulping cigarettes,
sucking in cathode rays,
I walk outside.
Just let me breathe,
that's all I want—
it's half a block before I even feel
boots on concrete
dusted with Brooklyn-Queens Expressway grit.
I try to look around
and can't, sensing through bronchi alone
clear cool oxygen.
The air is good today, thank god.
I charge ahead block after block,
the brownstones a blur of brown stone,
the trees vague leafing entities,
the cars anathema and shunned.
After five or six blocks my vision starts to clear—
there're the steps where I met Angeline,
there's the kid that ran in front of my car last week,
there's the corner where I first got lost—
Fort Greene real for a moment.
I'm heading south, a bit calmer now,
about to brave the traffic of Atlantic Ave.

And I do feel an odd bravery coming on,
facing part of what's kept me inside—
the metal and mindless motion and fumes,
this shrieking honking swerving impatience,
this Type-A drive to get and do and go, to move,
to thrust, to careen driven—this mess of mass.
I cross the churning gauntlet on a cloud—
I am untouchable because I will not touch.
I stay astride the noisy artery, Vanderbilt—
the very name suggests the overbuilt,
this cataclysm it takes so much to step beyond—
I'll stride this flesh through brick and glass,
through concrete and the door
to reach the park and soak in green.
Isn't that what this skin craves
through every goddamned pore—the breach of air,
the momentary clack, the stench of chlorophyll and mud.
Still a stretch to go, though,
and it's not these sooty storefronts that I wish to see,
the bullshit, the urge, the crackaday hustle
—so I start to think about walking,
and about how odd it is to think about walking,
and about when I first ever thought about walking,
about who first got me thinking about it—
could be Kerouac, could be Thoreau—
no, I think it was old man Tolkien,
great walker himself and writer of walking
who first gave me the thought, the gift of the thought
that one's own doorstep leads out to every road on Earth
—what was it?—*the road goes ever ever on*—
that being on the road is being home as well, is being.
And here I am, being, walking into Grand Army Plaza,

giant crazy whirlpool of cars, and I walk right in,
without breaking stride across five full lanes
up onto the center island
(and this no traffic island but a real island in traffic
with grass and trees and benches and a plaque
and the huge, gorgeous arch leading nowhere
but the center, ominous and enigmatic)
and down again across five more lanes to a promontory
of sidewalk, then across five more, all in stride,
without pause or hurry, without a single honk,
without a single oncoming vehicle to jar my pace
in what some might think a miracle but I see (at the time)
as just walking. I pause before the park in a coughing fit,
then enter in, eager as ever to bask, and head on up the path—
when the toxins kick in, every cell gushing
New York poisons to the blood—soot, monoxide, cigarettes,
pesticides, thick perfumes, cheap hamburger steroids, cheap beer,
spoiled food, lead chips, radium, and a thousand million farts
ratcheting the veins and soaking the nerves in some deep
hirsute panic—as I head on in, the park itself dims
and I can barely see past my mind—that tree I love
is leering like my last lover must when he thinks of me,
the cold-hearted bastard, and why is he still in my head,
why does the mind retain that which spoils, one time
I thought of a lost love for two years every time I tied my shoes,
not this tree, please, and there's the field but I can only think
of Boy Scout picnics with the stern adults, my father expecting
so much of me who could barely tie a knot, I couldn't tie
my shoes correctly till I was thirty-two (that's true), all these knots
the trees grinning scars of storms and drought and all the shit
of everyday life and yeah we all have scars so why should I care
so much about the grade school boys laughing at me for putting flowers in my hair

I put on a goddamned good school play didn't I thank god I've forgotten their names
and all those coked-up drunken nights with men I felt I couldn't fulfill
and the time I finally scored a touchdown in a game with the neighborhood kids
on my own front lawn running like mad and laughing unstoppable at last victorious
only to find I'd gotten turned around and scored for the other team
what a fucking dunce and I'm turned around now really disoriented
I've charged into a thicket up on some hillside I should be able to see
where I am but I'm surrounded by cranky six-foot bushes how'd I even get in
this fucking place in a deep adrenaline surge I crash right through
into an open stand of trees. There's a dull throb behind my left eye
and the sky's a bit too bright, the speckling new leaves are letting in too much
light in too many shifting patterns, I'm short of breath and that old black tooth
begins to sing they say I have my mother's teeth four pulled already
and three dying soon to be crunched and crumbled and spit in chunks
about my boots. So I stand staring at these old boots, beaten, scraped,
discolored old friends who've carried me many many miles,
and for the first time I wonder where they're from, I bought them
on sale six years ago at Strawbridge's, but really from
some sweatshop in Asia or Seattle maybe,
some underpaid worker churning them out,
leaking their own sweat into the leather
in that unpleasant boot-in-the-face mood of capitalism
you might call Bootism—Bootism, that's funny—
or might Bootism be something else entirely—
I think of that not-so-faceless worker's sweat in my boots,
and my sweat in my boots, and the countless moods and molecules
they've been through, and of how we invest ourselves in things,
instill our lives into the things we live with and through,
and I think: a good pair of boots are the Bootist's way.
I laugh. That's ridiculous—and of course it must be—
to live through your boots, to live by walking,
like Tolkien and Kerouac and Thoreau

who saw walking as living, life as a walk,
and I think: Shit, I started this walk in 1961.
I take a big suck of air and sigh it out,
and stand there breathing for a minute,
checking out the patterns of old leaves and new grass,
and how these oaks are really very happy today,
Spring is finally soaking in, the leaves rustle
very quietly and I think I can smell them,
the air really is marvelous today and I plunge
on down the hillside out onto the edge of my little field.
How did I feel so lost—right here all the time.
The sun is saturating this late April late afternoon,
and there's a bunch of little kids running and yelling
in some ruleless game, parents lounging on the grass,
and a biplane sputters overhead with a banner
saying— no shit— *Happy April!*—and I walk
back through the field feeling the new grass through my bootsoles,
and all the way home I have that rare state of mind
where I'm seeing things I've never noticed,
always in front of my face, always now seen—
my favorite tree has a carving of a burning heart;
at the entrance to the park two old Italian men sit
in their portable chairs, just sitting, as they sit every day;
in the Plaza a tree has an army of sparrows;
that building has almost sentient gargoyles bottom to top;
that botanica sells Breath of Jesus in a can;
that driver is wearing a bunny suit;
that man is mowing the sidewalk;
there's a woman showering in the car wash;
that house has Christmas decorations year round;
those steps are painted with a prayer to St. Francis;

the kid that ran in front of my car is signing to his mom;
the incense lady wears a button that says 59¢;
the corner deli's sign has a pig with a halo.
As I start back down my block,
I think once again of the two Bootisms:
Bootism—boot in the face;
Bootism—living through boots:
one I despise and one I live—
then I recall the grass I'd tromped
so gleefully in the late afternoon sun,
the new green breathing grass,
and wonder if it's really just a matter
of which side of the boots you're on.
The shadows are long.
The air's taken a chill.
I put my key in the gate,
hear the familiar clink of the lock,
and smell the musty entranceway.

Learning to Trust Your Gut

FRANCINE WITTE

Remember that first you are
an animal, reacting in animal
ways. Your nostrils flare at predators.
Your eyes squint you out of the sun.
Your body tells you everything. You know
all this. You've always known. But still,
you have doubts. You button a blouse
over a twinge in your belly, smooth lipstick
over a quivering lip. You teach yourself
to adjust. And when alarms go off,
blaring you out of a burning building,
you learn to breathe shallow, or step
around the flames. You know a lie
in a whisper, or taste goodbye
in a kiss. But you have magazines stacked
to the ceiling telling you to ignore
the flutter inside your bones. But listen,
your heart's in a cage for a reason. It's
a prisoner banging up against the walls,
scraping a cup along the bars,
just waiting for someone to hear.

JOEL ALLEGRETTI is the author of five collections of poetry, most recently *The Body in Equipoise* (Full Court Press, 2015), and is the editor of *Rabbit Ears: TV Poems* (NYQ Books, 2015). His poems have appeared in *The New York Quarterly, Barrow Street, Smartish Pace, PANK*, and numerous other journals worldwide.

ROGER APLON has written ten books of poetry, most recently *Improvisations*, and one prose collection. In the course of his career, he has been awarded many prizes and honors including an arts fellowship from the Helene Wurlitzer Foundation in Taos, New Mexico. Roger now makes his home in Beacon, New York, where he edits and publishes the poetry magazine *Waymark*.

WILL ARBERY is a writer, filmmaker, and theater-maker. His writing has appeared in *Better Magazine, The Awl, decomP, Word Riot, Neutrons Protons, D Magazine*, and more. He recently received the Claire Rosen and Samuel Edes Foundation Prize for Emerging Artists. Will is part of the Early Career Writers' Group at Clubbed Thumb, and the Kendeda group at The Alliance Theatre. His play *The Mongoose* was an *LA Times* "Critic's Pick." He has seven sisters.

MARCIA ARRIETA is the author of two poetry collections: *archipelago counterpoint* (BlazeVOX, 2015) and *triskelion, tiger moth, tangram, thyme* (Otoliths, 2011). She edits and publishes *Indefinite Space*, a poetry/art journal.

SUE HYON BAE is International Editor for *Hayden's Ferry Review*. Her work appears in *Four Chambers Presents: Poetry and Prose for the Phoenix Art Museum, Please Hold Magazine, Apple Valley Review*, and elsewhere.

SAVON BARTLEY is a North Chicago born poet, writer, and Oreo cookie connoisseur. Known for his lyricism and ability to command a crowd, he has worked with HBO Def Poets, United Nation officials, and Grammy, Oscar, and Tony Award winners. Savon's work is a reflection of his experiences with identity, mental illness, social justice, and what it means to be a man who is better than his father.

JOE BAUMANN possesses a PhD in English from the University of Louisiana at Lafayette. He is the author of *Ivory Children* (Red Bird Chapbooks, 2013) and his work has appeared in *Tulane Review, Willow Review, Hawai'i Review*, and *Jelly Bucket*. Joe teaches composition, literature, and creative writing at St. Charles Community College in St. Charles, Missouri.

GABRIELLA M. BELFIGLIO lives in Brooklyn with her partner and five cats. She teaches self-defense, conflict resolution, karate, and tai chi to people of all ages throughout the five boroughs. Gabriella's work has been published in anthologies and journals including *E·ratio, Literary Mama, Radius, The Avocet, Potomac Review*, and *Lambda Literary Review*.

ZOÉ BESMOND DE SENNEVILLE is a young Parisian author and actress. She likes to write as an actress is present onstage: without control, with her body, and with her blood.

CHANEL BRENNER is the author of *Vanilla Milk: A Memoir Told in Poems* (Silver Birch Press, 2014). Her poetry has appeared in *Poet Lore, Diverse Voices Quarterly, Muzzle Magazine, West Trestle Review*, and others. Her poem "July 28th, 2012" won first prize in *The Write Place at the Write Time*'s contest judged by Ellen Bass. Chanel lives in Santa Monica, California.

Born and raised in central New Jersey, **CAROL BROWN** is a performance poet, student, and general bookworm. She is currently studying poetry and psychology at Eugene Lang College. As a poet, she enjoys working cross-media, often performing with graphic and/or music to accent the spoken words. Carol has been featured at the New York City Poetry Festival, LaMama Experimental Theater, the 2014 TEDYouth Conference, Jersey City Slam, and on Indiefeed

PRUDENCE CHAMBERLAIN is a London-based experimental poet, focusing on feminism, queerness, and gender. Her poetry has been published in *3:AM Magazine, HYSTERIA, Lunar Poetry, Jungftak*, and most recently, as part of Indolent Book's *HIV Here & Now* project. A first collection is forthcoming with Knives Forks and Spoons Press. Prudence is a Visiting Lecturer in Creative Writing at Royal Holloway University, and Poet-in-Residence at Surrey University.

JOHN CLINTON was born and raised in Brooklyn. He has been published in *Nomad's Choir*, the great weather for MEDIA anthologies *The Understanding between Foxes and Light* and *I Let Go of the Stars in My Hand*, issues of NYSAI Press, and *Estrellas En El Fuego* from Rogue Scholars Press. John currently resides in Staten Island.

SHIRA DENTZ is the author of *black seeds on a white dish* (Shearsman), *door of thin skins* (CavanKerry), and the chapbooks *Leaf Weather* (Shearsman) and *Flounders* (forthcoming from Essay Press). Her writing appears in journals including *The American Poetry Review, The Iowa Review, jubilat*, and *New American Writing*. Her awards include an Academy of American Poets' Prize, the Poetry Society of America's Lyric Poem and Cecil Hemley Memorial Awards, and *Painted Bride Quarterly*'s Poetry Prize. Currently Shira curates *Drunken Boat*'s blog feature, "What I'm Reading Now," and teaches creative writing at Rensselaer Polytechnic Institute in Troy, New York.

ALEJANDRO ESCUDÉ's first book of poems, *My Earthbound Eye*, was published in 2013 by Sacramento Poetry Center Press. He holds an MA in Creative Writing from UC Davis and works as an English teacher. Originally from Argentina, Alejandro lives in Los Angeles with his wife and two children.

SARAEVE FERMIN is a performance poet and epilepsy advocate from New Jersey. She is editor-in-chief of Wicked Banshee Press, a contributing editor for *Words Dance*, and book reviewer for Swimming with Elephants Publications. Her first full-length book, *View From The Top of the Ferris Wheel*, is due out from Emphat!c Press in 2016 and her work can also be found in *Germ Magazine, Drunk in a Midnight Choir*, and the anthology *We Can Make Your Life Better: A Guidebook to Modern Living* from University of Hell Press. SaraEve believes in the power of foxes and self-publishing.

SARA FETHEROLF spent parts of her childhood in California, the Midwest, and rural New Jersey, so her writing is inspired by the odd dreamscapes and back-roads that make up this country. Her recent publications include poems in *Red Paint Hill*, *The Chattahoochee Review*, *Salamander*, *Turnip Truck(s)*, and *Hypertrophic Literary*. In Fall 2016, Sara will be attending the Creative Writing & Literature PhD program at the University of Southern California as a Dornsife Fellow.

CORNELIUS FORTUNE is a Detroit-based freelance journalist, editor, and playwright. His play, *Dislocations*, was selected for performance during the 2014 Thespis Festival in New York and was a finalist for the Downtown Urban Theater Festival. In 2015, Cornelius participated in Theater for the New City's Dream Up Festival with *Against Human Nature*; a retelling of the fall of man from the angel's perspective. He has written content for a Fortune 500 company, ghostblogged for a circus performer, won an award for enterprise reporting, and rebranded a popular emagazine.

CHRISTIAN GEORGESCU (Geo) is a writer, performer, and visual artist from New York City. Expanding on his previous solo productions *Meisner with Mama* and *iLucifer*, Christian is at work on his kaleidoscopic production, *The House of ME*.

BRENDAN GILLETT is a fall flavor. He usually avoids arguing on the internet, but is happy to throw his two cents at you in person. You can find him in various places doing various things, etc.

GEORGE GUIDA is the author of eight books, including four collections of poems: *Pugilistic* (WordTech Editions, 2015), *The Sleeping Gulf* (Bordighera Press, 2015), *New York and Other Lovers* (Smalls Books, 2008), and *Low Italian* (Bordighera, 2006). His poetry and fiction appear in *Alimentum*, *Barrow Street*, *Harpur Palate*, *Inkwell*, *Literature and Gender*, *Perihelion*, and other journals and anthologies. He co-edits *2 Bridges Review*.

JANET HAMILL is the author of six books of poetry and short fiction: *Troublante*, *The Temple*, *Nostalgia of the Infinite*, *Lost Ceilings*, *Body of Water*, and *Tales from the Eternal Café* which was named as one of the Best Books of 2014 by *Publishers Weekly*. Her seventh book, *Knock*, is forthcoming in 2016 from Spuyten Duyvil.

DEBORAH HAUSER is the author of *Ennui: From the Diagnostic and Statistical Field Guide of Feminine Disorders* (Finishing Line Press, 2011) and a contributing editor at *The Found Poetry Review*. Her work has appeared, or is forthcoming, in *Carve Magazine*, *TAB: The Journal of Poetry & Poetics*, and *Antiphon*. She leads a double life on Long Island, New York, where she works in the insurance industry when she isn't writing poetry.

KATIE HIBNER is a confetti cannon from Cincinnati, Ohio. Her poetry has been published, or is forthcoming, in *Bone Bouquet*, *glitterMOB*, *Modern Poetry Quarterly Review*, *Powder Keg*, and *smoking glue gun*. Katie has been a reader for *Salamander* and *Sixth Finch* and is a freshman at Bennington College. She would like to dedicate this publication to her mom, Laurie.

ANNA HOLMQUIST grew up in a small Wisconsin town and transplanted herself to the big city of Chicago a few years ago, where she performs many different kinds of things in many different places.

VICKI IORIO, a native New Yorker, lost her mind and moved to Florida. It wasn't witness protection but it sure felt like it. That being said, she's back in New York and will never leave again! Vicki is the author of the poetry collections *Send Me a Letter* (dancing girl press, 2016) and *Poems from the Dirty Couch* (Local Gems Poetry Press, 2013). You can also read her work in *Home Planet News, Five 2 One, San Pedro Review, Paper Street Journal, The Mom Egg*, and *Crack the Spine*.

As a journalist, **ERIK IPSEN** relishes the license that his fiction writing gives him to escape the fetters of hard reality and to make stuff up in the service of the story.

KHADJIAH JOHNSON is a writer and humor advocate reigning from Brooklyn. She is a Louis B Goodman Creative Writing nominee, the runner-up recipient for the 2015 NYC Youth Poet Laureate title, and her work has taken her to various festivals and institutions such as The Brooklyn Book Festival, NYU, Lincoln Center, National Black Writers Conference, plus her Off-Broadway comedy *Cozbi's Kitchen* was featured at the New York Live Arts Theater. You can catch her studying, and occasionally teaching writing workshops, at Brooklyn College.

KIT KENNEDY lives in San Francisco and is both *Bay Times* Poet-in-Residence and Poet-in-Residence of her church. She has five published poetry collections and owns an equal number of pairs of red shoes.

CRAIG KITE is a New York poet published in *Maintenant 9: A Journal of Contemporary Dada Writing and Art* by Three Rooms Press, and *Periscope* by NYSAI Press. He is also a visual artist and poet/vocalist in the band Heads on sticks.

RON KOLM is a founding member of the Unbearables and a contributing editor of *Sensitive Skin* magazine. He is the author of the poetry collections *The Plastic Factory, Divine Comedy, Suburban Ambush*, and (with Jim Feast) the novel *Neo Phobe*. A new collection of his short stories, *Duke & Jill*, has just been published by Unknown Press. In addition, his work can be found in *Hobo Camp Review, The Otter, Have A NYC 3*, and *The Outlaw Bible of American Poetry*. Ron's papers were purchased by the New York University Library, where they have been catalogued in the Fales Collection as part of the Downtown Writers Group.

PTR KOZLOWSKI has been a taxi driver, a deliveryman, a poet, printer, singer-songwriter, and guitarist. He likes to draw upon his experience to bring a musical perspective to the spoken word. Ptr's work can be found in journals and anthologies including *Hobo Jungle, Brownstone Poets, ANYDSWPE*, and *I Let Go of the Stars in My Hand* from great weather for MEDIA.

DAVID ROY LINCOLN is the author of a novel, *Mobility Lounge* (Spuyten Duyvil), and several poetry chapbooks including *The Interloper* and *By The Way*. He has published short fiction, poetry, and travel writing in numerous journals and newspapers, and received fellowships from the Virginia Center of the Arts and the Christopher Isherwood Foundation. His piece in this anthology is an excerpt from a forthcoming new novel, *The Bhakti*.

TSAURAH LITZKY is a widely published poet and writer of fiction, plays, memoir, erotica, and commentary. Her full-length poetry collections are *Baby On The Water* (Long Shot Press) and *Cleaning The Duck* (Bowery Books). Tsaurah's sixteenth chapook, *Full Lotus*, is due out in summer 2016 from NightBallet Press. She hosts THE RESISTANCE reading series at Gallery Gaia, Brooklyn.

RICHARD LORANGER is a writer, performer, visual artist, and all around squeaky wheel, currently residing in Oakland, California. He is the author of *Sudden Windows* (Zeitgeist Press, 2016), as well as *Poems for Teeth*, *The Orange Book*, and nine chapbooks. Recent work can be found in *Oakland Review*, *Dryland*, *Overthrowing Capitalism vol. 2* (Revolutionary Poets Brigade), and the online anthology *HIV Here & Now*.

m.nicole.r.wildhood's essays and poetry have appeared, or are forthcoming, in *Lodestone*, *The Mighty*, *The Atticus Review*, *Ballard's Journal of Street Poetry*, *Pankhearst*, and *Litro Magazine*. She currently writes for Seattle's street newspaper *Real Change* and is at work on a novel and two full-length volumes of poetry.

KATHARYN HOWD MACHAN, author of thirty-two published collections (most recently *Wild Grapes: Poems of Fox* from Finishing Line Press), is Professor of Writing at Ithaca College. In 2012 she edited *Adrienne Rich: A Tribute Anthology* (Split Oak Press).

MARY MACKEY is the author of seven collections of poetry including *Travelers With No Ticket Home* and *Sugar Zone* (winner of the PEN Oakland Josephine Miles Award), plus fourteen best-selling novels including *The Village of Bones*; a prequel to her critically acclaimed Earthsong Series. Mary's literary papers are archived in the Sophia Smith Special Collections Library, Smith College, Northampton, Massachusetts.

LIV MAMMONE is an editor and poet from Long Island, New York, where she lives with her parents, brother, family of feral cats, and geriatric dachshund. She has previously taught creative writing at Hofstra University and Queens College. Her poetry has appeared in *wordgathering*, *Rogue Agent*, *Wicked Banshee*, *QDA: A Queer, Disabled Anthology*, and is forthcoming in *Grabbing the Apple*, and *Typo Magazine*. Liv was the winner of Union Square Slam's 2015 Nerd Slam. She is the third visibly disabled poet ever to place as a finalist for a national slam.

NATASHA KOCHICHERIL MONI is a first-generation American of Dutch and Indian descent. Born in the North and raised in the South, she finds home in the Pacific Northwest. Natasha's first full-length poetry collection, *The Cardiologist's Daughter*, was released by Two Sylvias Press in 2014. Her writing has been published in journals including *Magma*, *Luna Luna*, *PANK*, *Hobart*, *Rattle*, and *Indiana Review*.

DAWN Z. MONTEFUSCO has published poetry in *Bellingham Review*, *Gargoyle*, *Clark Street Review*, and *Minetta Review*. She received her BA in Writing from New York University and her MFA in Creative Writing at The Inland Northwest Center for Writers. Dawn grew up in the Bronx but currently lives in Portland, Oregon, where she works as a writer and life coach.

MIKE MORAN lives in Mount Vernon, Iowa. He is a writer, director, actor, schoolteacher, and also plays, sings, recites poetry, and tells stories on behalf of the Iowa Goatsinger.

LINDSY J. O'BRIEN has an MFA in Creative Writing from Minnesota State University, Mankato, where she also teaches writing. She owns Red Step Press, a small nonfiction press, and her own creative work has appeared in various local and national publications.

WILLY PALOMO learned poetry from the worlds of hip-hop and slam poetry. In 2015, he received his BA in English and Creative Writing and an Honors degree from Westminster College in Salt Lake City, Utah, where he founded the college's first poetry slam team and served as Editor-in-Chief for *ellipsis*. He has competed nationally as a member of Salt City Slam and Westminster Slam. His work is published, or forthcoming, in *Muzzle*, *Vinyl*, *HeArt Online*, and elsewhere. Willy is currently pursuing an MFA in Poetry and MA in Latin American and Caribbean Studies at Indiana University.

PUMA PERL is a widely published poet and writer, as well as a performer and producer. She is the author of the full-length poetry collections *Retrograde* (great weather for MEDIA, 2014) and *knuckle tattoos*, and the chapbooks *Ruby True* and *Belinda and Her Friends*. Puma is the creator, curator, and producer of Puma Perl's Pandemonium which brings spoken word together with rock and roll. As Puma Perl and Friends, she performs regularly with a group of excellent musicians. She is also a journalist and writes cultural and arts columns for *The Villager* and other publications. Puma is a recipient of a 2016 Acker Award in New York City.

VIVIAN FAITH PRESCOTT is a fifth-generation Sámi-American, born and raised on the small island of Wrangell in Southeastern Alaska. She is the founding member of Blue Canoe Writers in both Sitka and Wrangell with an emphasis on mentoring Indigenous writers. Vivian lives at her family's fishcamp in Wrangell. She was a Joy Harjo Award semi-finalist, received Honorable Mention in *Boulevard*'s Poetry Contest for Emerging Writers, and was awarded the Jason Wenger Award for Literary Excellence. Vivian is the author of one full-length poetry collection and two chapbooks. Her short story collection is forthcoming from Boreal Books.

JILL S. RAPAPORT's collection of fiction, *Duchamp et Moi and Other Stories*, was published in 2014 by Fly by Night Press/A Gathering of the Tribes. Her work has appeared in publications including *Resister*, *Global City Review*, *Big Bridge*, *Sensitive Skin*, *Found Object*, and *The Williamsburg Observer*. Work of hers can also be found in the anthologies *Up Is Up, But So Is Down: New York's Downtown Literary Scene 1974-1992* (NYU Press, 2006), and *The Outlaw Bible of American Poetry*.

Everyone in This Movie Gets Paid, DAN RAPHAEL's nineteenth book, will be published in summer 2016 by Last Word Press. His poems have appeared recently in *Otoliths*, *Caliban*, *Big Bridge*, *Phantom Drift*, and *Rasputin*.

GAYLE RICHARDSON is a writer and proud crazy cat lady who spends her free time writing poems, just like her late Grandpa, Donald. She has been published in *I Let Go of The Stars in My Hand* (great weather for MEDIA, 2014) and currently lives in Suffolk, England. When she isn't busy speaking her mind, Gayle enjoys sharing precious moments with the most important man in her life—Paul.

TODD ROBINSON's poems have appeared in *Chiron Review*, *Arc Poetry Magazine*, *Sugar House Review*, *Natural Bridge*, *Midwest Review*, and elsewhere. His first volume of poetry, *Note at Heart Rock*, was published by Main Street Rag Press in 2012. Todd teaches in the Writer's Workshop at the University of Nebraska and in various arts organizations.

SOODABEH SAEIDNIA was born in Iran and received a PharmD and PhD in Pharmacognosy from Tehran University of Medical Sciences. She has written roughly 150 scientific papers for various academic journals, as well as books in both English and Farsi. Now living in New York with her husband and son, she is a freelance researcher. Soodabeh's poetry is published, or forthcoming, in *Sisyphus Quarterly*, *TimBookTu*, *Her Mind Rocks*, *Bobbling Irrational*, *The Dwells of Minds*, and many others.

ANNIE SAUTER is a poet and spoken word artist from Colorado and upstate New York. She has been published in multiple anthologies and has a chapbook published by Bright Hill Press. She began writing in the 1960s in the underground and women's presses in New York City and the Bay Area of California and has performed all across the United States.

CECILY SCHULER is a 2016 MFA candidate at the Pratt Institute in Writing and Social Activism in Brooklyn, New York. A 2013 Bread Loaf Writers' Conference contributor in non-fiction, Cecily's work has been published or is forthcoming in *Wicked Banshee*, *Fairy Tale Review*, *Ellipsis*, *Duende*, and *Fire Stories: Further Thoughts on Radically Rethinking Mental Illness*. Cecily has been teaching, collaborating, and performing on stages across the country since 2009. They are the current slam manager at Union Square Slam in the heart of every New York City Monday.

JARED SINGER is an audio engineer and poet living in Brooklyn. He has represented New York eight times at the national slam level including two final stage appearances at the National Poetry Slam. He is a five-time New York City Grand Slam Champion and his work has appeared in *The Legendary, Union Square, Huffington Post*, and more. He writes frequently about his favorite things in the world: science, comic books, and love. Jared Singer believes in the healing power of kittens, whiskey, and listing things in groups of three.

JOHN W. SNYDER is a poet from Staten Island who loves words.

JAN STECKEL's poetry collection *The Horizontal Poet* (Zeitgeist Press, 2011) was a winner of a 2012 Lambda Literary Award. Her fiction and poetry chapbooks, *Mixing Tracks* (Gertrude Press) and *The Underwater Hospital* (Zeitgeist Press), have also won awards. Jan's creative writing has appeared in publications including *Scholastic Magazine, Yale Medicine*, and *Bellevue Literary Review*. She lives in Oakland, California.

TAYLOR STEELE is a Brooklyn-based spoken word artist, playwright, and essayist. She received her BA from The New School, has been published by online publications including *Apogee Journal, HEArt Journal, Blackberry: a magazine*, and is a content writer for *The Body is Not an Apology*. Taylor placed fifth in the 2015 Women of the World Poetry Slam and sixth in 2016. She believes in the power of art to change, shape, and heal.

PHILLIP STERLING is the author of the short story collection *In Which Brief Stories Are Told* (Wayne State University Press); the full-length poetry collection *Mutual Shores* (New Issues); and four chapbook-length series of poems, the most recent of which, *And for All This: Poems from Isle Royale* (Ridgeway Press 2015), is a selection of poems written during his Artist-in-Residency for Isle Royale National Park, Michigan.

CHRIS STEWART is a functional meta-reprogrammer of human bio-computers, a poet, and a life coach. His work has been anthologized in *Break-Out: A Calling Card From The Rising Stars Of The Tees-side Scene* (Ek Zuban, 2013). Chris lives in Yorkshire, England, and is presently converting his life into a text-based adventure. Hear him at the Cheltenham Literary Festival in 2017.

SB STOKES is creative like a starfish has arms. He writes, draws, designs, produces, and edits in Oakland, California. His first book of poetry, *A History of Broken Love Things*, was published by Punk Hostage Press in January 2014. A chapbook of SB's poems, *DARK ENTRIES*, was also published in October 2014 by Gorilla Press and The Pedestrian Press. A fourth-generation Californian, SB is one of the founding producers of Uptown Oakland's free, annual literary festival, Beast Crawl.

ED TONEY is a Brooklyn poet and chemist. A longtime participant in Louis Reyes Rivera's workshop in Brooklyn, Ed also frequents workshops at Cave Canem, and reads all around the city.

Originally from Monterey, California, **AJ URQUIDI** has studied poetry in Los Angeles and New York City. His poems have appeared in such journals as *Chiron Review*, *Foothill*, and *Thin Air*, and won the Gerald Locklin Writing Prize. He has led creative writing workshops at CSULB and Beyond Baroque in Venice Beach. AJ currently lives in Long Beach where he co-edits the online writing journal *indicia*, and investigates grammar for the *Los Angeles Review of Books*.

CHRIS WIEWIORA grew up in Warsaw, Poland, where his parents served as Evangelical missionaries under the Iron Curtain after they completed cross-cultural training in Los Angeles. He earned an MFA in Creative Writing and Environment at Iowa State University. His nonfiction has appeared in *Best Food Writing 2013*, *Gastronomica*, *RE:AL*, *Slice*, and many other magazines.

JOHN SIBLEY WILLIAMS is the editor of two Northwest poetry anthologies and the author of nine collections, including *Controlled Hallucinations* (2013) and *Disinheritance* (forthcoming 2016). A five-time Pushcart nominee and winner of the Philip Booth Award, American Literary Review Poetry Contest, and Vallum Award for Poetry, John serves as editor of *The Inflectionist Review* and works as a literary agent. Previous publishing credits include: *The Midwest Quarterly*, *Third Coast*, *Baltimore Review*, *Nimrod*, and *Bryant Literary Review*. He lives in Portland, Oregon.

MAW SHEIN WIN is a Burmese American poet, editor, and educator who lives and works in the Bay Area. Her writing has appeared in various journals including *Eleven Eleven*, *Cimarron Review*, *Ping-Pong*, and most recently, the anthology *Cross-Strokes: Poetry Between Los Angeles and San Francisco* (Otis Books / Seismicity Editions). She is a poetry editor for *Rivet* and was an Artist-in-Residence at the Headlands Center for the Arts in Sausalito, California. Her chapbook, with paintings by Mark Dutcher, *Ruins of a glittering palace*, was published by SPA / Commonwealth Projects. She is a member of the San Francisco Writers' Grotto.

FRANCINE WITTE is the author of the poetry chapbooks *Only, Not Only* (Finishing Line Press, 2012) and *First Rain* (Pecan Grove Press, 2009), winner of the Pecan Grove Press competition, and the flash fiction chapbooks *Cold June* (Ropewalk Press), selected by Robert Olen Butler as the winner of the 2010 Thomas A. Wilhelmus Award, and *The Wind Twirls Everything* (MuscleHead Press). Her poem "My Dead Florida Mother Meets Gandhi" won first prize in the 2015 Slippery Elm Poetry Award. A former English teacher, Francine lives in New York and is an avid iPhoneographer.

EMMA WOOTTON gained her MA in Poetic Practice from Royal Holloway University, and has most recently been accepted for publication in Reward Publishing's 2016 Global Social Justice anthology. Her work appears in *Glitterwolf Magazine* and *Articulus!*, anthologized in publications from Loose Muse, Angle Grinder, and great weather for MEDIA; and was commended in the Mother's Milk 2014 Writing Prize. Emma lives in Manchester, England.

OLIVIA WU's poems have appeared in *Aberration Labyrinth*, *Shen Jiang Weekly*, and *First Literary Review-East*. She is a member of Brevitas, an invited community of poets. She is also part of Poetry Society of America's poetry workshop group. Olivia resides in New York City.

Born in Moscow, Russia, **ANTON YAKOVLEV** studied filmmaking and poetry at Harvard University. He is the author of the chapbooks *Neptune Court* (The Operating System, 2015) and *The Ghost of Grant Wood* (Finishing Line Press, 2015). His work is published, or forthcoming, in *The New Yorker*, *Fulcrum*, *American Arts Quarterly*, *Measure*, *Blue Monday Review*, and elsewhere. Anton has also directed several short films.

BRENDA YATES grew up on military bases. After Tennessee, Delaware, Florida, Michigan, Massachusetts, Japan, and Hawaii, she settled first in Boston, then Los Angeles. Her poems appear in publications including *Mississippi Review*, *City of the Big Shoulders: An Anthology of Chicago Poetry* (University of Iowa Press), and *The Southern Poetry Anthology, Volume VI: Tennessee* (Texas Review Press). Awards include the Beyond Baroque Literary Arts Center Poetry Prize, a Patricia Bibby Prize, and honorable mention in the Robinson Jeffers Tor House Poetry Contest. Tebot Bach published her first collection, *Bodily Knowledge*, in 2015.

great weather for MEDIA

Founded in January 2012, **great weather for MEDIA** focuses on the unpredictable, the bright, the dark, and the innovative. We are based in New York City and showcase both national and international writers.

Visit our website for information about our weekly reading series, events across the United States and beyond, submission calls, publications, and to sign up for our newsletter and blog.

Website: www.greatweatherformedia.com

Email: editors@greatweatherformedia.com

Twitter: @greatweatherfor

Facebook: www.facebook.com/great.weather

Instagram: www.instagram.com/greatweatherformedia

MORE

great weather for MEDIA titles

ANTHOLOGIES

The Careless Embrace of the Boneshaker

Before Passing

I Let Go of the Stars in My Hand

The Understanding between Foxes and Light

It's Animal but Merciful

COLLECTIONS

John Paul Davis, *Crown Prince of Rabbits* (forthcoming)

John J. Trause, *Exercicises in High Treason*

Wil Gibson, *Harvest the Dirt*

Corrina Bain, *Debridement*

Aimee Herman, *meant to wake up feeling*

Puma Perl, *Retrograde*

CPSIA information can be obtained
at www.ICGtesting.com
Printed in the USA
FFOW05n0005120716